CREATIVE
WELLNESS

CREATIVE WELLNESS

THE POWER OF THE
PERSONALITY TO HEAL SELF

Michelle Lusson, D.D.

The Printed *Voice*

The Printed Voice
98 Main Street, No. 538
Tiburon, CA 94920

Cover Design: *Greg Whitrock*
Text Design: *Tori Hernandez*

Library of Congress Cataloging-in-Publication Data
Lusson, Michelle.
 Creative wellness : the power of the personality to heal self / by
Michelle Lusson.
   p. cm.
 Previously published in 1987 with subtitle: A stress-management
guide to total health happiness.
 ISBN 0-9637891-2-0 : $11.95
 1. Stress (Psychology)—Prevention. 2. Personality assessment.
3. Health. I. Title.
RA785.L87 1994
613—dc20   94-2787
                CIP

Printed in the United States of America
10 9 8 7 6 5 4 3 2 1

CONTENTS

Foreword by Patricia Aburdene, author of *Megatrends for Woman*

PART I

PART II

PART III

ACKNOWLEDGMENTS

I WISH TO TO THANK MY SISTER, Dottee Mella Nuckols, for making this book a possibility. Simultaneously, my gratitude goes to Leslie Keenan, editor and publisher, and to my close friend, Susan Drescher-Mulzet, for creating the way for it to reach the public. NIMO and I thank you!

FOREWORD

NEVER MIND YOUR ASTROLOGY SIGN. What is your god or goddess type? Are you an Iris, possessing psychic abilities but prone to hypertension? An Eros, who should eat six small meals each day, especially when under stress? A Venus, who should surround herself with vibrant reds and pinks? A Mercury, who needs to take time off from work and sail around the Bahamas?

Discovering which of fourteen gods and goddesses fits your individual personality is your key to a dynamic and revolutionary new program of wellness maintenance for inner and outer health and beauty.

The Creative Wellness Plan is unique because it combines a sound health plan with pioneering New Age therapies such as color healing, meditation, gem support, and aromatherapy.

When I took the program ten years ago, weight balancing was my main focus. But I soon discovered that weight loss was only the beginning. When I began the program, I discovered that my blood pressure was surprisingly high. Eight weeks later, it registered a perfect 120/80. My complexion glowed, my self-confidence grew, and I was finally learning how to manage stress. If you're a person who does not need to lose weight, you will still want to follow the Creative Wellness principles to produce other benefits, including reshaping the body without losing weight. Besides, Creative Wellness is fun.

Learning the character traits of your god or goddess provides fascinating and practical insights into your own personality. Discovering the right colors for your wardrobe can enhance your image and well-being. Through modern gem therapy you can find that wearing the right gems can alleviate a headache, clarify your thinking, even increase your stamina.

The Creative Wellness Plan addresses the total person—physical, mental, emotional, and spiritual. I learned how supportive the spiritual component can be while following the program myself. In my case, I ate whatever I liked for a short time but began to meditate daily. I soon discovered the strength to discipline my eating habits. While meditating, I burned the incense of my goddess type and lit the color of candles indicated to support my personality's transformation.

One would expect the creator of this unique plan to be an extraordinary and unusual person. She is! Reverend Michelle Lusson founded Creative Wellness as a result of thousands of individual lifestyle counselings. She is inwardly inspired and is dedicated to the health and well-being of humanity. Employing both intuition and logic, Michelle has cooperated with many physicians to help compose a system that would assist people in solving their health problems and realizing their full human potential.

By studying the effect of what a natural health plan does for a person, she has discovered a fascinating relationship between the psyche and the body's chemistry. She calls it "bio-psychology." Through stress, poor diet, and negative attitudes, people can upset their natural chemical balance, which can cause illness. To repair the possible damage and prevent disease, you must follow a well-balanced nutritional program, learn to manage stress, and develop a positive outlook on life. That's the sum of the Creative Wellness Program. It sounds simple, but it can be the greatest challenge of a lifetime.

As a reader, how do you know which type you are? A simple diagnostic test at the beginning of the book has been specially designed by Michelle Lusson to determine your god or goddess type. You can also use this test on your family and friends.

The timing of *Creative Wellness* is perfect. There is a new respectability for addressing the total person. A growing segment of the public is now willing to accept that good health has its roots in emotional and spiritual well-being.

Even corporations, which are often considered conservative in matters like these, are turning to wellness programs to cut the high cost of corporate health care. My husband, John Naisbitt, and I cited the Creative Wellness Plan as an innovative new model in self-help care in one of our best-selling books, *Re-inventing the Corporation. Creative Wellness* is a revolutionary how-to book, a whole new approach to color, a compendium of pioneering new therapies. It is a total lifestyle maintenance program.

You will use the Creative Wellness Plan in your home, in your office, and in your leisure time. Long after you finish reading, it will continue to support you; you will never forget that you are a god or goddess!

Patricia Aburdene
Co-author of *Megatrends for Women*

PART I

CHAPTER I:

YOUR MIND
BODY RELATIONSHIP

I MAGINE. YOU ARE IN GOOD physical condition. You are in touch with your own needs; you weigh exactly what you want to weigh. You are never overly fatigued or depressed, never have insomnia, high blood pressure, headaches, backaches, allergies, asthma, rashes, chronic stomach distress, or ulcers. You always feel in control, productive, and certain of your goals.

This may seem to describe the perfect man or woman, but it could be you! Unfortunately, none of us feels good all the time, but most of us don't realize how capable we are of tuning in to ourselves and having an impact upon our own health—partly because we don't understand how stress affects our autoimmune responses. All the illnesses above can be caused by our reactions to stress. Stress, when out of control, can affect one's entire lifestyle adversely.

You have the power within yourself to conquer stress physically and emotionally. You can triumph over it by changing any destructive attitudes or behavior patterns in your personality. You can resist stress by having a good nutritional program, by personalizing an exercise regime, and by learning to use your natural sensitivity to strengthen your defenses. You can improve your mental and emotional health by knowing how to relax and how to enjoy your leisure time. All this and more can be accomplished by understanding yourself and who you are.

THE MIND
BODY CONNECTION

The most important aspect of the Creative Wellness Self-Improvement Program is that it focuses on you and your personal needs. It aids you in taking responsibility for your own health maintenance. For this reason, the key to Creative Wellness is understanding your personality and how it affects your health. Discovering your personality dynamics—how you act and react—is the first step to psychological health. Why? Because you have a fundamental mind/body connection.

Creative Wellness not only offers you a simple list of health improvement suggestions, it gives you a complete lifestyle program to follow. It will help you to stay balanced even when an unexpected stressful situation occurs, such as losing your job or the death of a loved one. During these times it's imperative that you know how to stay in control of yourself, body, mind, and spirit, for total health maintenance.

Creative Wellness is a holistic lifestyle plan for self-maintenance. It begins with personality typing, followed by positive self-projection (reinforced by meditation and affirmation), and personalized meal planning and good nutrition, along with toning and balancing exercises. Natural supports, such as wardrobe colors, gemstones, scents, and oils are factored into one's individual plan for extra energy and support. All these self-help tools are personalized according to your specific personality needs. They will strengthen you, physically and emotionally, improve your self-image, and reinforce your innate character traits. They will help you to get in touch with yourself and your needs in the best way possible in order to cope better with life's problems.

The basis of the Creative Wellness Plan is the mind/body connection. The endocrine system, which forms the principle bridge between the mind and body, is its starting point. The endocrine system consists of all the ductless glands in the body. These glands are responsible for the production and performance of the hormones that keep the chemistry of the body in balance. This complex system is affected by thoughts, feelings, and emotional reactions that send messenger cells via the central nerve network, positively or negatively, to all areas of the body. Thus, when a person identifies how their personal glandular vulnerability can affect their physical reaction to stress, such as the common headache, it is, for them, the first step in learning how to heal the self.

Since thoughts and feelings express one's personality, it's easy to see how a person's mind can affect their internal chemistry. In turn, an innate glandular imbalance can alter the development of a healthy personality. In other words, identifying a glandular vulnerability will exhibit a personality's strength or weakness.

GLANDULAR TYPING

How can you discover your unique personality/glandular vulnerability? How does this knowledge reveal your innate weaknesses? Your strengths? The Creative Wellness testing method is simple! All of your glands have focal points in your body at which the nerve cells responsible for passing messages from the brain to the glands are centered. By testing these points through muscular responses, and by seeing which ones respond weakly or with strength, you can discover your personality/glandular type.

This muscle test, which I call a personality categorizing test, is based on the alternative science of applied kinesiology, a method of assessing neurological responses by interpreting automatic muscle reflexes. Dr. John Diamond pioneered this testing of behavioral habits with muscle kinesiology in the late 1970's. He determined whether his patients were in discord or harmony with themselves (*Your Body Doesn't Lie*, Warner Books, 1987). The Creative Wellness system has taken his test one step further to determine a personality type through glandular-muscular testing.

Once you take the test, you're ready to learn about your personality and about the power you have within yourself to commence your total healing. This testing of neurological points, relative to your glands, will reveal your innate glandular vulnerability, stemming from heredity, early life conditioning or wrong choices made in adolescence. By the time you're 21 years old, you may have established an undermining glandular weakness that can be affecting your personality and influencing your total health. How to take the personality test so as to discover your personal glandular vulnerabilities will be elaborated upon in Chapter II.

EAST MEETS WEST

I know that this handbook will serve as a comprehensive introduction to total self-help care. Even though Creative Wellness focuses mainly on combating stress, its philosophy is to encompass the caring of the whole person—mind, body, and spirit. The theory behind the system was developed after 25 years of counseling and working with more than 12,000 clients. My background in spiritual psychology and interdisciplinary research led me to realize that the human body is truly "the temple of the living spirit." This was the driving force behind my developing a self-help system where an individual could take responsibility for their daily health maintenance.

Following a personal near-death experience, my life was changed. What I discovered from this trauma was that inside every human being there are two distinct natures existing simultaneously: the spiritual and the physical. What connected these two natures together, and what sustained life, were the two queries that prompted me to look into the connection between philosophy and alternative methods of healing.

These questions led me on a personal spiritual journey and eventually to the development of my Spiritual Psychology and Creative Wellness courses. I researched the wisdom behind healing of ancient cultures, particularly as it pertained to a dual nature. Each religious philosophy I examined was separate and distinct, but all shared a similar attitude toward spiritual healing: a belief that the spirit is housed in the body, and both the laws of the spirit and the laws of the body must be acknowledged. In other words, each human has a spiritual and a primal nature, and both must be addressed in health. After a trip to India and numerous encounters with other therapists, I became convinced that one of the main bridges between mind and body was the endocrine system. I discovered that glands were the singular link between Eastern and Western practices of healing. And, I knew that I had found a key to the blending of the inner spirit with the mind/body connection for health.

Hindus believe that a person has a soul made up of subatomic energy (that is, the energy of or relating to particles smaller than the atom), and held in structural form by energy vortices called chakras. These chakras correspond exactly with the pattern of the endocrine system. Within these chakras there exists a spiritual blueprint for one's life experience. This spiritual mapping interacts with the physical life force found within the DNA of the body's cellular structure. Together, these separate patterns influence a person's psychological disposition and physical chemistry, as the chakras combine the spiritual intelligence of the soul with the growth patterns of the body—hence life itself!

Western understanding acknowledges that the intelligence of the body can be measured through three systems: the central nervous system, the autoimmune system, and the endocrine system. When a person is subjected to too much stress, the energy of one of these systems is disturbed, and health can be adversely affected. Creative Wellness combines both these Eastern and Western philosophies; so that when a gland is not functioning up to par, the life force of the whole person is affected, and both health and performance can suffer.

After further research at a foundation that combined a group of professionals in alternative health fields, I was led to design a system that incorporated a new form of psychology—one that addressed the spiritual and physical interpersonal relationships. Individuals with certain glandular vulnerabilities appeared to have similar personality traits, which corresponded to their glandular weakness. The opposite was also true; a strong gland often indicated an inherent strength of character. Simplifying this extensive research, my associates and I established a system of fourteen basic personality types, seven male and seven female, so as to document a health-care program. Each personality type concurred with one or more glandular influences. When subjected to continued duress (a negative form of stress) without treatment, these innate weaknesses could surface as symptoms of either a physical or psychological illness, or both.

THE PERSONALITY TYPES

The Creative Wellness System was born. The fourteen personality types were formed into one of three major categories, depending upon the gland most affected by stress: the Thyroid, the Adrenal, and the Pancreas. There are four Thyroid personalities (two male and two female), four Adrenal types (two male and two female), and six Pancreas types (three male and three female). Each of the seven male personalities relates similarly to a female type with parallel glandular vulnerabilities. But even though similar, there are distinct differences, partly due to different psyches between men and women, and partly due to different hormones produced on the sexual level.

We named the fourteen personality types after gods and goddesses. Although this concept is popular today, we were pioneers some twelve years ago in identifying different personality types with Greek and Roman gods and goddesses. The significance of archetypes in humankind's psyche is attributed to Carl Jung, the father of modern psychology. He believed in a collective unconscious with a set of archetypal images common to all people. He felt that these ancient belief systems affected the progression of humanity on both a conscious and an unconscious level, and contributed to both culture and social architecture in their evolutions. Thus, memory of the past can be a source of learning, as well as inspiration today, when brought to conscious awareness. Also, turning to past Greek and Roman deities is fitting because these personas of power represented both divine and human qualities.

In the Creative Wellness Plan, the name of an ancient god or goddess is assigned to each personality type. This identification provides the archetypal image. Most importantly, it helps to inspire the person to start on a self-improvement program. It's exciting to identify with a god or goddess and to find one that shares your personality. Since the mythical deities are both earthly and spiritual, they can represent your dual nature without threatening your religious beliefs. Their earthliness was vulnerable, but their divinity had the power to create change. You too, are subject to human frailties, but capable of preventing many of them when you learn to control your stresses.

You may notice that some of the deities chosen are Roman, and some Greek. In a few instances, the deity that we assigned for personality profiling is Greek rather than its Roman counterpart because of the different ways the two ancient societies viewed each deity's distinct characteristics. In order to make a bridge from myth to modern psychology, we chose the particular one that fits the contemporary personality of today's man and woman, such as Athena, the trendsetter, and Apollo, the diplomat.

HOW TO USE THIS BOOK

This book contains the entire ten-step Creative Wellness Plan. The program is explained at length in Chapter III, which should be read before you read about your personality, as it will explain how you can best incorporate this knowledge into your psyche. In order to determine your personality type, turn to Chapter II, which explains glandular typing. From there you can turn directly to your personality type found in Part II. All the Creative Wellness supports will be found there, except nutrition, which has been grouped separately into Part III.

CREATIVE WELLNESS

Years ago, when we originally designed the health maintenance system, few reports were being published on the negative effects of stress on health. However, a small incident convinced me that I could wait no longer to take our specific guidelines for stress management from the research foundation into the marketplace. I had just finished eating at my favorite restaurant in Northern Virginia and was talking to the waitress, a young woman who had taken one of our nine-week courses in weight-management. She was so pleased with herself—she had lost twelve pounds, felt great about the way she looked, and she no longer felt stressed or fatigued on the job.

A business executive, one of her regular customers, was seated a short distance away and overheard our conversation. He asked if the program could help him and his employees—not to lose weight, but to learn how to handle stress correctly. The company that he owned was a small high-tech company and was looking for solutions to job-related stress. "Can you teach someone like me to handle stress more effectively?" he asked.

Today, as I look back on this simple request twelve years ago, I recollect on the now thousands of clients who have benefited from the many diversified classes. From every situation imaginable, clients came—from housewife to college student, from corporate mid-level manager to air traffic controller, as well as many psychotherapists and other health-care providers. Even though their backgrounds differed, their needs were the same: better health and freedom from the negative effects of stress.

Stress management is a vital part of health maintenance. We have seen countless clients reduce blood pressure, control allergies, improve digestion, rid themselves of headaches and backaches, and improve their self-esteem. My associates and I have witnessed many individuals creating new lifestyles for themselves and actually achieving what once seemed impossible goals.

You too can have this power. You can learn how to control your life's problems by learning simple disciplines in self-awareness. You can begin to recognize your individual sensitivities and discover how to treat them naturally through supportive alternative methods of self-help care. Once you determine your god or goddess archetypal personality, you will be on your way to a program to create a new you!

CHAPTER II:

FINDING YOUR DIVINE
PERSONALITY

B EFORE YOU CAN LEARN to employ the self-improvement
tools designed specifically for your personality, you must discover
your god or goddess type. As mentioned in Chapter 1, there are
fourteen Creative Wellness personality types, and these fall into three major
glandular groupings. The fourteen personality types are briefly illustrated
in Figure 1.

You are now ready to discover your archetypal persona. You will refer
to yourself throughout the rest of the book by this deity's surname. The first
step is to find out which of the three glandular categories fits you; that is
your major glandular type. The second is to discover which divine personality fits you under that category. In other words, if you are a woman who
falls into the thyroid type, you will want to know whether you are an Artemis
personality or an Athena. The two-part kinesiology test will tell you.

To take the complete personality kinesiology test you need only find
someone other than yourself to be the tester. Anyone can test or be tested
with a little practice if the following procedure is followed correctly.

Figure 1 • Goddesses and Gods Shown According to Types

GODDESSES

Thyroid Types

Athena

Artemis

Adrenal Types

Iris

Venus

Pancreas Types

Minerva

Aphrodite

Diana

GODS

Thyroid Types

Apollo

Mercury

Adrenal Types

Neptune

Bacchus

Pancreas Types

Atlas

Eros

Hermes

Discovering Your Major Glandular Type

1. Stand up and face your tester, touching nothing for support, with your right arm at your side and your left arm extended, as shown in Figure 2.

Figure 2 • How to Type

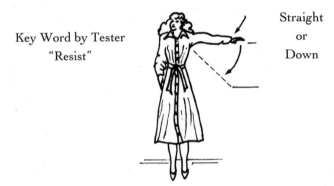

Key Word by Tester
"Resist"

Straight
or
Down

2. Your tester should practice testing your left arm's resistance by placing his or her right hand over your wrist. Upon giving the command "Resist," the tester should try to push your arm down gently with a quick spring-like motion. It is the strength or weakness of your arm's resistance that determines the strength or weakness of the gland touched by your tester.

3. Have your tester study the points of the body drawn in Figure 3 that correspond to the three major glands. To discover which of the major categories you belong in, your tester will check your responses to the stimulation of these three nerve points, moving from the thyroid point to the pancreas to the adrenal in Figure 3. The major gland nerve circuits of your body can be tested accurately only if the thyroid is tested first, then the pancreas, and then the adrenal. (This is different from the actual order that the glands appear in your body, from the head to base of the spine.)

Figure 3 • Glandular Checkpoints

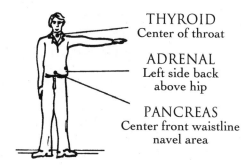

THYROID
Center of throat

ADRENAL
Left side back
above hip

PANCREAS
Center front waistline
navel area

4. On the thyroid point, the tester should use the thumb and index finger of their left hand to lightly touch the center of your throat. Simultaneously, the tester uses their right hand to press your extended arm down with a gentle spring-like motion while giving you the command, "Resist."

5. To check the pancreas point, the tester places the index and middle finger of her or his left hand slightly to the left of your navel, a few inches below your ribs. Again, the tester checks your arm's resistance with the word, "Resist."

6. Now, for the adrenal point, the final major glandular point, using the left thumb and index finger, the tester reaches around to your back and gently touches an area directly above your hip pad in the small of your back. Again, while giving you the command, "Resist," the tester attempts to press your arm downward.

The test should reveal a weaker response in one of the three nerve glandular points. Your first weak response at any major point will determine the category where your personality typing will be found.

If your tester finds only strong responses to each of the three major points, you need to call to mind any recent stressful situation; then repeat the test. Remember, stress weakens the body's energy system and will clearly show where your vulnerabilities lie.

The next step for your personality typing is to discover which of the deities fits you best in your glandular category. Follow the same testing procedure while looking at Figure 4.

Figure 4 • *Corresponding Glandular Points*

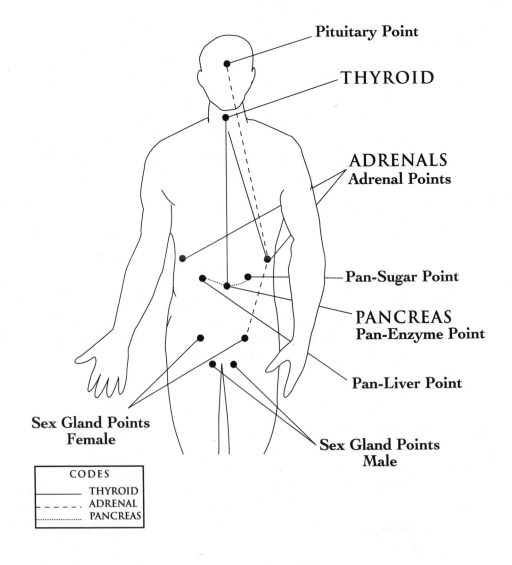

DISCOVERING YOUR PERSONALITY TYPE

Thyroid Personality Types

If you are in the thyroid category, you are either an Artemis or Athena, if a woman, or a Mercury or an Apollo, if a man. To determine which one of these personalities matches you the best, your tester must check two more minor points on your body that correspond to either your adrenal or your pancreas—the reason being, you have an inherent connection between the thyroid and adrenal, or between the thyroid and pancreas. These reflexes correlate with your early personality development. Your body will now show the minor weakness at one of these points according to how you respond to stress or outside stimuli.

To check

1. Check the pancreas reflex first as in the original testing. This point is in the center front at the waistline near the navel area. The tester gives the command "Resist." If you test weak at this point, you are either an Artemis or a Mercury personality type and can proceed to your program.

2. Now, if you did not weaken at the pancreas point, go on and have the adrenal point checked by your tester. If you weaken there, you are either an Athena or an Apollo. If both points check strong, think of recent stress and repeat the test.

Adrenal Personality Types

If you are in the adrenal category, you are either an Iris or Venus, if a woman, or a Neptune or Bacchus, if a man. To determine which archetypal personality you are, your tester needs to check two more minor glandular points; one relative to the pituitary gland (whose nerve point lies in the middle of the forehead) and one relative to the sex glands. (See Figure 4 for exact points for testing.)

1. To check the pituitary nerve reflex, the tester should use only the index finger to touch the center of your forehead slightly above your eyebrows. Give the same command as used for testing the major category, "Resist." If this point is weak, you are either an Iris or a Neptune, and are ready to proceed with your self-improvement plan.

2. If the pituitary was not weak, your tester needs now to check the sex gland reflex. For women, this nerve point is in the middle of the lower abdomen and can be located by the tester using the thumb and index finger, holding them about four inches apart. This point is related to the ovaries and if weak, you are a Venus. For men, the nerve point is slightly lower, and lies just above the pubic bone. If this root point is weak, you are a Bacchus.

3. For the adrenal archetypal goddesses or gods, if no minor points show vulnerability, you need to think of things that stress you, and be checked again.

Pancreas Personality Types

If you are in the pancreas category, you are either a Minerva, an Aphrodite, or a Diana, if a woman or an Atlas, an Eros, or a Hermes, if a man. To determine which of these personality types fit you best, your tester must check three more minor nerve points on your body relative to total function of the pancreas. These are pan-sugar, pan-enzyme, and pan-liver, as they represent the action of metabolism and the seat of the emotions.

1. To check these reflexes, the tester begins with the pan-sugar nerve point located at the waistline, just under the left rib area, using the index and middle fingers to touch this point lightly while giving the command, "Resist." If your arm weakens here, you are either a Minerva or an Atlas, and you need test no further.

2. To check the pan-enzyme nerve point, your tester, using the same fingers as above, need gently touch a point at the center of the waistline, immediately above your navel. If this point shows a weak response, you are typed as an Aphrodite or an Eros.

3. The last point to check for pancreas personality typing is the pan-liver nerve reflex. This point is also located at the waistline, but this time on the right side of the body just below the rib cage. If you show a weak response here, you are a Diana or a Hermes. As before, if you tested strong on all three pancreatic points, you might recall an emotional situation that was upsetting to you; then be tested again.

Secondary Personalities

If you have been typed as a particular god or goddess and are in the process of making a change in your life, you might appear to be another god or goddess were you to be retyped. Do not be alarmed. You are not changing your primary archetype, but rather are adding an expanded dimension to your reality. This expansion is called a secondary personality.

As in the Myers/Briggs Type Indicator™ and other psychological assessment systems, secondary personality traits can show up when one is making, or has recently made, a particular lifestyle movement. In Creative

Wellness, this principle also holds true, as most individuals can have a secondary or shadow personality. The secondary personality usually complements the primary, rather than opposes it. One can therefore assume that this other self is being called upon to provide extra support during a changing or stressful period.

To work with your secondary, take from its profile the inner strength that would reinforce your innate character. Do not concern yourself with the health vulnerabilities related to this secondary, as these weaknesses seldom create an illness. Your primary type's inherent glandular vulnerability is usually the root cause for your problematic health conditions, be they emotional or physical. The secondary personality surfaces at times to emphasize a psychological need in you to pay attention to a softer, more loving, or even stronger side of your nature, which you might have overlooked when making a lifestyle change.

Now that you know your primary glandular personality typing and have found your goddess or god surname, you are ready to begin to learn how to use the individually designed Creative Wellness tools to claim your own power to help yourself.

CHAPTER III:

THE CREATIVE
WELLNESS PLAN

T HE FIRST STEP IN ACHIEVING your Creative Wellness
goals is to understand your personality. Your true character may
be a mystery to you, so hidden perhaps that your potential strengths
have remained unrecognized and unused for years. As you begin to understand yourself, you will find your life taking on new clarity and purpose.
You will feel a power within yourself to heal and change your life.

The first step, then, of the ten-step Creative Wellness Plan, is to understand your personality and why you do what you do. Since all good healthy
habits start in the personality, this will help you to move forward to the
other steps. Each step will train you to improve a specific area in your lifestyle.
You may follow them in the order given, as many clients and students have
preferred in the past, or you can choose selectively the ones that resonate
most to your needs. For instance, you may already have a good nutritional
program given to you by your health-care provider and don't need a new
one. Instead, you can begin with your wardrobe planning.

Following is a list of the ten steps, with a general description of each and
their importance to your health and well-being. You will find these head-
ings repeated throughout your own personality section. Refer back to this
chapter for specific information on how to proceed.

YOUR TEN-STEP CREATIVE WELLNESS PROGRAM

STEP I:	*Understanding Your Personality*
STEP II:	*Reprogramming Your Psyche*
STEP III:	*Creating Healthy Nutrition*
STEP IV:	*Color Support in the Wardrobe*
STEP V:	*Gem and Stone Strengthening*
STEP VI:	*Scents, Herbal Elixirs, and Oils*
STEP VII:	*Hobbies and Interests*
STEP VIII:	*Exercise for Glandular Improvement*
STEP IX:	*Divine Relationships*
STEP X:	*The Inner Power — Meditation*

Step I: Understanding Your Personality

Begin your Creative Wellness Plan by studying your personality profile to become familiar with yourself and your archetypal deity within. On the initial reading, you'll probably be too busy recognizing similarities between yourself and your goddess or god, and too surprised at finding yourself so clearly reflected in your deity's profile, to do much more than acknowledge the resemblance. However, reading the profile a second time will give you a chance to understand your personality dynamics. Once you view your personal strengths and weaknesses, you can laugh at certain of your behavior patterns that conceivably are amusing to you instead of painful, and you can feel pleased about qualities in yourself that you never appreciated. Most of all, you can now use this self-knowledge to commence a change in your personality in order to deemphasize a shortcoming in yourself that you've always wanted to be free of.

To gain mastery of your personality, you must study the lists of strengths and weaknesses in Step I that follow your goddess or god profile. These will be listed directly under the description of your specific goddess or god typing. Make note here that you should spend more time studying your strengths and less with your weaknesses, as your thoughts are carried by messenger cells to all parts of your body, and too much time spent on the negative short-circuits your energy system. You can refer back to your personality description whenever you are under stress and need greater understanding of yourself, or when you are having problems being motivated to take care of yourself.

Step II: Reprogramming Your Psyche

Since self-discovery is your path to good health, you are now ready either to cultivate a positive personality trait that you did not immediately recognize in yourself or alter a negative one that may be creating stress.

This process is called behavior modification. This stage involves your learning two behavior-modification tools: affirmation and sensory stimulation, that include a reconditioning affirmation along with incense and candle burning.

The purpose of the affirmation is to retrain your thought patterns. All affirmations are written in sonnet or poetic style, so as to stimulate both hemispheres of your brain, while helping you to deemphasize early life conditioning that no longer serves you in your adult life. You will find your personalized affirmation immediately following your strengths and weaknesses. If you desire, you can check the effectiveness of the affirmation on yourself by testing your major glandular reflex, as you did when discovering your typing. You will note that your reflex has strengthened. So, the more you say your affirmation, the stronger you become, and the more power you have to overcome your shortcomings.

The other behavior-modification discipline is sensory stimulation, which includes your personalized scents and a ritual of candle burning using individually designed color candles for your typing. This therapeutic tool cultivates in your emotional response system the stage for positive thinking gained by your affirmation. Scents and visual imagery send direct signals to your brain. Therefore, your personalized scents and colors are devised as sensory enhancers to motivate and inspire your mind and heart. In my research, I found that the burning of incense and the lighting of candles have been used in ritual since ancient times to calm and aid a person to become more receptive to positive reinforcement.

In addition, the candle colors are associated with qualities that can strengthen you, and these too are listed with your candle colors. Because each personality type is unique and complex, the same color can affect each goddess or god differently. The colors can help you focus on the positive attribute that helps to diminish any of your personality weaknesses. As with the affirmation, if you want to check your reflexes to measure your benefits, have your tester check you again after you have lit your candle for half an hour.

For the greatest benefit, light your candle, burn a stick of incense, and say your affirmation three times. Leave your candle lit for a half hour.

The benefit to be gained from your overall behavior modification is self-realization. In childhood, you were conditioned to respond in certain ways to certain situations. These responses can help or hinder you, depending on whether they increase or decrease your ability to cope with stress. It is helpful here to identify your child within. Is it a happy, well-adjusted adolescent or a child in need of support and healing? If the latter is true, don't blame your parents, but consider your own feelings today and find a buddy to do the program with you so you can mirror your progress and take control of your own existence.

Time after time, I have seen clients come to understand their own weaknesses and use this knowledge to transform their lives. A student of mine came to me to find a solution to her asthmatic problem. She had tried numerous medical treatments with no success and had finally decided that her problem was self-induced. By studying her Iris profile, she found that she had not been nurtured sufficiently by her parents when she was a child and repressed her ability to attend to her personal needs. Confronted with this self-knowledge, portrayed in her personality weaknesses, she immediately began to support the inner child within with affirmations and greater sensitivity to her needs. Her dark blue, green, and white candles aided her to feel stronger in herself. Her scents of rose and jasmine strengthened her adrenal reflex, and she quickly discovered that she could control her own asthmatic reactions and forgive her parents for their lack of awareness of her childhood need for love.

Step III: Creating Healthy Nutrition

Now that you have discovered how your personality makes you susceptible or resistant to illness, you are ready to learn how different types of foods can either protect you from or leave you vulnerable to poor glandular function. In your Creative Wellness Plan, you will start with guidelines specific to your personality typing that include a selective diet, unique to your glandular needs; priority foods, supportive to your energy requirements; and limited and avoidance foods, detrimental to your health. (Note that the nutrition step is listed separately from your personality section, in Part III.)

When planning a balanced diet, you should always choose foods that are compatible with your digestive assimilation capabilities. Since a person's metabolism is controlled by their endocrine performance, one type of diet is recommended for a particular goddess or god typing, but not for the others (although goddesses and gods in the same glandular categories do have the same nutritional needs). For example, the personalities that are thyroid-gland vulnerable require extra protein in their nutrition plan, including red meat; while those with an adrenal predisposition need to watch their cholesterol levels and limit their intake of red meat.

There is also a vitamin and mineral requirement list for each goddess and god type in order to provide the needed additional supplements for improved health and reduction of ill effects from stress.

Meal timings are listed, as well, to help you decide the best times to eat, and how often. People with thyroid vulnerabilities, for instance, handle their largest meals best in the middle of the day, since their energy levels slow down by the evening hours. These personality types should try to eat before 10:00 pm to ensure better assimilation of food and less stress on the endocrine system.

After your meal timing order, you will find specific suggestions or daily instructions that will reinforce your new eating habits. For example, the adrenal types require a relaxed environment for at least one of their meals a day, for if they eat when hurried, their food does not assimilate properly. For the pancreas types, they should avoid eating when emotionally stressed, as they might experience indigestion after the meal.

The last section of your individual nutritional plan can be especially helpful if you are watching your weight. Although weight loss is not the object of this book, being overweight can cause stress in any individual. Therefore, weight-loss instruction is an important ingredient in the nutrition chapter for goddesses and gods.

I have designed a weekly menu plan that labels the first three days as "weight loss," the next three, "weight maintenance," and the seventh day, "fun day." These are sample menus of what you can create for yourself depending upon whether you want to lose, gain, or maintain your weight. For example, create a three-week, weight-reduction menu counting your calories as given on the "weight loss" three-day plan, and then repeat the meal planning for another three weeks until you start to show improvement. If you are more than twenty pounds overweight, see your physician before starting any diet.

The most important part of the Creative Wellness nutritional guidance is taking responsibility for your own health care. If you study your nutrition plan found in Part III, you will find at the end of each chapter "Creative Meal Planning Techniques," "Preparation Hints," and "Suggested Substitutions." Remember, there are no limits on how imaginative you as a god or goddess can be when you create good meal planning for yourself, your family, and your friends when entertaining them. There are wonderful cookbooks in bookstores today that offer stress-free recipes for health, if you understand your own basic nutritional needs first.

Step IV: Color Support in the Wardrobe

After teaching yourself behavior modification and good eating habits, the next three steps of the Creative Wellness Plan offer you natural supports that can help improve your energy—the first being color energy.

Color used for healing has been around since ancient Egyptian times. The virtues of color support were extolled by the Greek physician/philosophers, Democritus and Aristotle. Moving forward in time, some of the most dramatic examples of color therapy were documented by a second-century Roman physician, Galen. He observed visible changes in a patient's body in response to color. Viewing all diseases as the result of blocked nerve channels, Galen set up screens to refract rays of light so as to create the full spectrum. He then used specific colors of the rainbow to unblock the nerve passages to aid patients' healing.

My introduction to color as a healing tool was very personal, in that it was introduced as the power of color, a nonverbal human response, by my sister, Dorothee L. Mella, author of *The Language of Color* (Warner Books, 1988) and the as yet unpublished *Colors for Healing*. Her work in color effect, both psychological and physical, aided me in the developmental phase of the Creative Wellness Plan. I often conferred with her on combining the arts for living with philosophy and science. Could a color palette be created that would support inherent glandular weaknesses, while giving added energy to a person when under stress? By having my clients wear certain colors and then testing their reflexes, I discovered a pattern—a consistent pattern of color response, that of cause and effect.

Certain colors weakened an already weak response; other colors strengthened the same response, and other colors prevented the originally weak response from appearing weak under any conditions. Time and time again, it was clear to me that colors had a definite effect upon people's glandular vulner-abilities and a positive effect on their personalities when being supported by the same. For example, the thyroid personality types can wear all shades of blue well, but must be careful when wearing certain shades of red, as these red hues can increase stress levels of these particular goddesses and gods. On the other hand, the adrenal types require red in the wardrobe for energy support during periods of stress.

To guide you in selecting your wardrobe colors, I have divided the sup-port colors into categories, based on whether they provide balance, secu-rity, inspiration, or protection.

The balancing colors are those essential to the everyday wardrobe, to be worn in suits, dresses, and so on. These colors help maintain energy stability throughout the whole working day.

The securing colors support the emotional well-being of the wearer and are best worn in coordinate items—blouses, shirts, etc.

The protection colors guard the wearer from outside stresses, particu-larly when the person is at risk, and should be worn when participating in sport activities, and in coats and other outer gear.

The inspiring colors help to stimulate creativity and are ideal for all creative and romantic pursuits. These can be used in both formal and casual attire, but not for long, long, periods of time, as they offer little energy protection, but are always uplifting.

Finally, Creative Wellness introduces color avoidance as a health dis-cipline. The approach is two-fold; first, there are certain colors that will adversely affect personality and its ability to resist stress; and secondly, even though not yet proven medically, the same avoidance colors could hinder an already innately impeded endocrine function. Based on our extensive research, each goddess and god has her or his own individual color chart showing the balancers, securers, inspirers, and protectors. Along with these support colors, the chart also lists the principle avoidance colors. For those of you who have quickly discovered that one of your candle colors for sensory stimulation in Step II is the same color as your main avoidance color—this is true. This color represents a weak trait of your personality, one that you are now, hopefully, willing to change into a strength. Designing a new wardrobe can be fun. Also, it will make you feel good to pass on to someone else the clothes in your avoidance colors, knowing that they can wear them with pleasure.

You may be wondering whether you can wear your favorite black, white, or gray outfits. By all means, these colors are the basics in wardrobe planning and may be worn with any color in your goddess or god color chart. The color black strengthens or reinforces the energy of the spectrum color worn, white reduces or dilutes the effectiveness of the color, except when specified on the palette, and gray neutralizes or tones down the action of the color energy. All patterns, such as stripes, flowers, dots, and checks, can be worn, but for greater support during periods of stress, it is best to go to your solids or plain colors.

Step V: Gem and Stone Strengthening

Like colors, gems and stones have had a prominent place in history as therapeutic tools. One of the oldest medical encyclopedias, the Papyrus Ebers, compiled in ancient Egypt around 1500 B.C., cites innumerable uses of gems and stones in the treatment of disease. A physician who practiced medicine in China during the Ming dynasty, 1400 A.D., also wrote about a pharmaceutical drink mix called the "divine elixir of jade" widely used to strengthen muscles, harden bones, calm the mind, and purify the blood.

A much more recent publication, *Stone Power*, also by my sister, Dorothee L. Mella (Warner Books, 1988) cites many examples of gemstone legends associated with psychological and physical healings. Hebrew priests, for instance, wore breastplates of semiprecious stones to protect themselves from evil and illness, as well as to inspire divine wisdom and intuition. Across the oceans, American Indians similarly used turquoise to give themselves hope and protect themselves from discouragement or despair. Crystals, for example, were used by most ancient healers, Tibetan physicians and Incan medicine men alike, to improve vision and cure eye ailments. Although I had been interested in using gems and stones in the Creative Wellness Plan for many years, associating them with their specific healing power and at the same time, determining which worked best for what personality type, took years of trial and error. Even though the ancients attributed many miraculous cures to the interaction between gemstones and people, I could not verify these as having actually occurred. Selecting gems and stones for each god and goddess personality out of the hundreds in existence was not going to be easy, but after years of research, I can now rely on my own experience. You may find this convincing too!

I discovered the healing power of amber, for instance, when I was giving a seminar on natural self-help care near Charlottesville, Virginia. During the seminar, a 40-year-old woman with a long history of allergies asked if we would try some Creative Wellness methods on her. She had attempted unsuccessfully to cure her severe headaches and other sinus symptoms with prescribed drugs and over-the-counter medications.

Through the kinesiology testing method used for typing the personality, it was determined that she had a weakness in her adrenal energy reflex. I recalled that I had read about the positive effects of organic and fossilized gems on the adrenal glands. By chance, we had a large piece of uncut amber among the stones that I had brought with me, and I suggested that she test the stone's effect.

Unbelievable as it may sound, this woman's symptoms were almost immediately relieved simply by holding the amber. Within a small amount of time, her nasal passages opened, and by the end of the seminar, her headache had disappeared.

Since then, I have witnessed hundreds of similar cases in which clients' symptoms disappeared or improved when they held or wore a particular gem or stone. Whether it is the stones' innate mineral properties that the body needs to regain its balance, whether it's the energy emitted by the gemstone itself, or whether in some way the stone triggers an archetypal memory or inner force for healing, I can't say with certainty. It may even be a combination of all three properties. But, whatever the interaction may be, it is my experience that it works and can be used as an adjunct with other forms of self-health care.

As each god and goddess has a different personality, the stones do have somewhat different effects on each type's psyche. For example, a brown jasper, a common earth stone associated throughout time with strength, gives the Mercury personality emotional stability, while for the Bacchus, a red jasper gives greater physical endurance. Similarly, amber protects the sensitive Iris against allergic reactions, but supports the Athena in coping with outside stresses.

The gems and stones selected in the Creative Wellness Plan are all semi-precious and can be obtained relatively inexpensively at most rock shops and department store jewelry counters. Goddesses can wear them in necklaces, rings, bracelets, pendants, earrings, belt buckles, or simply carry them in your purses. Gods can wear them in tie tacks, cuff links, belt buckles, rings, bolo ties, or tote them in your briefcases or pant pockets in small pouches. Your gems and stones will even help you when you are not actively thinking about them. All you have to do is to carry them somewhere on your body or place them in your home or office no farther than three feet away from you.

Learning to appreciate the natural energy from stones of the earth not only for their beauty, but for their supportive help as well, will be a rewarding experience. Considering the time required for them to form—millions of years for some—you can't help but appreciate them. In addition, wearing or carrying gemstones that generate wellness and foster feelings of well-being will increase your thankfulness of nature, as well as improve your appearance and good health.

Step VI: Scents, Herbal Elixirs, and Oils

The last natural support recommended in the Creative Wellness Plan—the use of scents, herbal elixirs, and oils—is the most inclusive, as it affects sensory stimuli. These nutrients of the earth affect you directly and indirectly by stimulating or calming your nervous system, hence, your emotional well-being.

Scents affect your self-image by making you feel more attractive and confident in yourself. Herbal elixirs (that is, pure essential oils derived from herbs) mixed in with soap, shampoo, body and hand lotions, or cologne and shaving lotion can make you look and feel healthy as they restore your energy and help you relax. Oils improve the quality of your skin, making you look and feel younger and more alive, as well as protecting you from many environmental stresses. Both can be found in health food stores and drugstores.

These same essences, especially the scents, can help you to alter your moods and frame of mind, as has already been proven in aromatherapy. It is for this reason that you were instructed in Step II, "Reprogramming Your Psyche," to burn particular flavors of incense when you recite your affirmation. By helping you lift your attitude, certain scents will aid you in becoming more receptive to a positive change—so call your scents your change agents.

As with color and gemstones, the use of scents, herbal elixirs, and oils is not new. Alabaster vessels from Egypt, dating as far back as 3,000 B.C., show traces of scented oils. Excavations of the ancient tombs and analyses of the artifacts found therein have revealed the use of oils in both cosmetics and medicines. In his book, *The Art of Aromatherapy* (Inner Traditional International Ltd., 1977), Robert B. Tisserand cites examples of healing with scents and oils not only in Egypt, but in other ancient civilizations as well.

He describes how Moses, in Exodus, was commanded by the Lord to make an apothecary ointment and was given specific instructions regarding the content and use of the holy oil. He also stated that Greek and Roman physicians recognized aromatic plants, especially flowers, as excellent for both sedatives and stimulants. Marestheus, a renowned Greek physician, used both the rose and the hyacinth to restore health to people with physical or mental symptoms of exhaustion.

Even today, the use of scents in medicine is being researched. A friend of mine from New England, Dr. Jerome L. Krasner, is primarily involved in researching the use of scents and odors in anesthetic masks for children. His investigation has shown that scents have a nerve-calming and stress-reducing effect in patients.

In the alternative therapies, such as the Bach Flowers remedies and the Perelandra Flower Essences, the use of elixirs from plants and flowers has been discovered to create positive effects upon the human emotional system. In Creative Wellness, we extended our studies to the exploration of the effect of essences on gland-related personality weaknesses or strengths. We detected a definite correlation between particular fragrances and certain personality types. For instance, a Neptune with a low tolerance to stress because of his inherent adrenal weakness, requires a musk scent to stabilize the pH balance in his skin to prevent hives, itching, or eczema, which are often his physical reactions to stress. He might use musk in either his soap or aftershave lotion.

Another combination of scent and oils working together was proven to me by a 43-year-old Minerva who came to class with one complaint of weight gain, but was demonstrating another: a low self-image and little or no motivation to improve self. We discussed her problem: first, her personality type's vulnerabilities and second, the nutritional plan that would strengthen her pancreas. We recommended she use plant elixirs that could rejuvenate her, thus motivating her to improve her looks. She would be able to find these in most cosmetic centers—herbal scents of jasmine and patchouli in soaps and bath oils, and aloe and Vitamin E in skin creams. Within weeks, this Minerva's attitude about herself changed. She had lost weight and improved her skin texture. She looked and appeared younger than her years and was very pleased with her new image.

You, too, can incorporate your natural support essences into your daily lifestyle. Stroke yourself by taking herbal and oil perfumed baths; pamper your skin with lotions containing your elixirs and oils; and wash your hair and body with soaps, gels, and shampoos of one or more of your scents, elixirs, and oils. They will work in tandem, not in conflict. Your personalized natural cosmetics will aid you to improve your state of mind, make yourself look and feel better, and be able to handle daily situations with more stamina. These gifts of nature can improve your health both physically and psychologically, as they have supported human life since the beginning of its existence.

Step VII: Hobbies and Interests

Planning recreation and leisure time is an important step in Creative Wellness, as it gives you the benefit of the right use of your time for relaxation and play.

To help you plan your leisure time, we have compiled a list of hobbies and activities that, based on your personality type, are most likely to appeal to you and, at the same time, benefit your health. The optimal use of your free time to give yourself physical and emotional release from stress, as well as to bring forth your personal strengths, is one of the best ways designed to improve your psychological health. Some of the hobbies and activities listed under your typing have been selected simply to help you release built-up tensions, while others will help you to improve your resistance to outside pressures. Some of these activities you may never have tried before, and although they seem to have little appeal, they can build your defenses against negative duress.

For some goddesses and gods, the hobbies and interests are competitive, for other types the activities give a sense of being in control. The creative ones, such as pottery-making and playing musical instruments, will encourage your self-esteem; the mental games, such as playing bridge and video/computer games, will enhance your intellectual faculties; the physical ones, such as baseball and scuba diving, will aid you to release tension and support your body's rejuvenation. The emotional ones, such as caring for plants and antique collecting, will stroke and reward you.

There are personality keys above each goddess and god chart that explain to you why you require certain kinds of interests. Read how your particular outdoor or indoor activity gives you the power to stimulate your creativity and challenge your skills. You may enjoy a new interest, something you have never experienced before. Invite your family, friends, and coworkers to join and play with you, for their health and happiness too.

Step VIII: Exercise for Glandular Improvement

The serious use of exercise for health improvement is no longer a new phenomenon. For many years exercise was considered helpful only for improving muscular strength and endurance, but now it is an important tool for total health. Disciplined exercise can reduce the risk of heart attack, lower blood pressure, reduce obesity, increase bone strength, and contribute to the prevention of such diseases as osteoarthritis, diabetes, and kidney problems. Exercise is important for people of all ages, even the elderly and infirm, who can enter into a simplified exercise regime that does not exceed their physical limits: walking, stretching, and breathing.

In designing Step VIII of the Creative Wellness program, we consulted with chiropractors, physical therapists, and dance instructors as well as Yoga, T'ai Chi, and martial arts teachers. Together we found that thirty minutes a day at least three times a week of any of the multiple disciplines would strengthen the glandular vulnerabilities. We also came up with exercises that relieve the specific stresses of each glandular type. The recommendations given for each god and goddess are not meant to take the place of a total exercise regimen, but can be easily incorporated into your regular routine. Suggestions are also given on the type of exercises your personality type will enjoy.

Daily exercise is an important part of your wellness plan. Like behavior modification and good nutrition, disciplined exercise requires responsibility for yourself: you set aside time each week for visits to the health spa, the community swimming pool, the biking trail, and the aerobics or martial arts class. When these activities do not fit your busy schedule, you should learn to do your exercise at home. You can acquire an exercise bike, a dance or workout video, a T'ai Chi tape, or even expensive Nautilus equipment.

In addition to setting time aside for exercise, you wear comfortable clothing, right for the exercise activity: such as, leotards for aerobics, stretch pants or tights for biking, and sweat outfits for walking around the block. Finally, in preparation for a beneficial program, you should never exercise on a full stomach, as your blood goes to digestion instead of muscle tone, and can put stress on your heart.

The thyroid personality types—Athena and Apollo, Artemis and Mercury—all require head, neck, and shoulder exercises, as they carry their tension in the upper portion of the body. For toning muscles, the areas that they should pay particular attention to are the chest, the upper arms, and the abdomen. To foster relaxation, it is necessary that they learn how to breathe properly. Their specific exercises are divided into four categories: glandular strengthening, overall toning, relaxation, and rejuvenation. Some of these routines include: head, neck, and shoulder rolls; push-ups, chest openers, and Yoga shoulder stands. For overall glandular improvement, they need to move the whole body, with activities such as jogging in place, aerobics, or running the mile.

The adrenal personality types—Iris and Neptune, Venus and Bacchus—all require stretching exercises that encourage good circulation, and hip and pelvic strengtheners, for stress causes them to lose their energy and libido. For toning muscles, the areas that these types need pay attention to are, for the men, their chests, and for the women, their hips. The men are prone to heart and lung ailments and the women to all the lower abdomen problems, including bladder and female organ dysfunction. Their exercises are divided into three categories: warm-ups, toning, and deep relaxation. Some of these routines include stretching and loosening up the whole spine through specific spinal flexor warm-ups, followed by dancing or jumping on a trampoline, or participating in swimming or water aerobics for cardiovascular improvement. For deep relaxation, they should learn creative visualization techniques where they see the life-force energy flowing to every cell of their body.

The pancreas personality types—Minerva and Atlas, Aphrodite and Eros, Diana and Hermes—all require torso, stomach, hips, and thigh toning, as they are affected by stress in the midsection of their bodies. To improve muscle tone, the areas that they should pay particular attention to are their waistlines, hips, and lower abdomens. Their exercises are divided into four categories: warm-ups, tummy tighteners, spinal flexors, and relaxation for digestive improvement. Some of the routines to follow include warm-ups of stretching the whole body, jumping jacks, Tummy Tighteners of sit-ups and knee-to-chest and leg exercises, Spinal Twist exercises, and dancing to music with a beat. For relaxation, the pancreas types require deep relaxation disciplines while they direct their healing power to their midsections.

As you begin your exercise program, it is important that you understand your limitations. Unless you are already exercising daily, you need to be patient with your progress. Only by improving your body's shape gradually and steadily can you achieve the toning and the rejuvenation your physical self requires. Remember that your body is the temple of the living spirit, and you want to keep it in the best shape possible, so as to live a healthy and productive life.

Step IX: *Divine Relationships*

Many clients, having completed the Creative Wellness Plan for themselves, want to know which god or goddess is compatible with their personality type. Since all of us seek harmonious relationships, we desire a level of compatibility with each of our loved ones. Demonstrations by scientists using Kirlian photography have shown kinetic energy force fields flowing from one human hand to another, exhibiting attraction or rejection. Where discordant, the auric energy fields repelled; where there was harmony between two individuals, the energies interfaced or blended.

In the last ten years, Stanford University, seeking health benefits created by positive human interaction, discovered healing could be accelerated by cohabitation of hospital patients of both sexes. Their research showed that male and female mixing had a distinct beneficial effect upon the total healing process.

Since our system is built on the wellness theory of "how the personality affects health," we deduced that one's personality could have an unseen effect upon another's chemistry—either positively or negatively. Again, through applied kinetic testing, we proved that there were compatibilities between the gods and goddesses, whether or not they knew one another before hand.

Today, there's a great interest in all areas of human relationships—in the workplace, in the community, and in the home. It's important for you to know: Can you work stress-free with your bosses or coworkers? Do you flow well with your emotional partner, and can you be a good parent to your child? Do you have to make some changes in yourself? Creative Wellness may have some of the answers. Our program has nothing to do with any form of astrology, nor the Myers/Briggs Type Indicator™ personality test;

what it gives is a more fruitful understanding of how your personality's innate strengths and weaknesses match or oppose another's.

For example, if you, as an Athena, are married to a Neptune, your relationship of personality compatibility is good, although not excellent, for you are both very independent individuals. You can work together on finding areas of interest that you both enjoy, such as horseback riding, an independent pleasure for each.

As an Eros, you get along best in all areas of life with your opposite, Aphrodite. Not true for some of the other archetypes who need to look for different women in work relationships than in romance.

Look up your compatibility chart. See which god or goddess you can have the best romance, friendship, or work relationship with. From your own strengths and weaknesses, recognize the sensitivities in another, and if they are not always to your liking, see where you could foster a better relationship. Ultimately, all individuals can get along together, but sometimes, this harmony requires a little extra give and take to promote and support another's growth and understanding.

Step X: The Inner Power – Meditation

The final and perhaps most significant step in the Creative Wellness Plan is the one that awakens your inner power: meditation. Many clients seeking health benefits from the wellness alternative methodologies have been surprised to learn the importance of deep relaxation followed by meditation so as to better cope with stress. The long-term health benefits are too many to enumerate: deep relaxation lowers blood pressure, reduces the risk of heart and lung problems, improves assimilation and elimination, and, most important, relieves worry, anxiety, and stress.

Eastern religions for thousands of years have taught meditation as a means of achieving inner peace. Today, Transcendental Meditation and the Zen disciplines are widely accepted in many stress-management programs for the corporate executive, as well as the air traffic controller. A person burdened with worry and anxiety lacks the inner peace necessary to obtain his or her goals, whereas a tranquil individual is mentally prepared to achieve what he or she wants, with little effort or waste of energy. Meditation, like exercise, should be practiced once a day. Ten minutes is sufficient, a half hour is better.

Meditation Exercise

To meditate you should follow these seven basic steps:

1. Find a quiet area or corner of a room where you will not be disturbed. Near you, place a favorite religious or spiritual object, such as a statue, a crystal, or a mandala.

2. Sit on a straight-backed chair with your feet firmly planted on the floor, or sit cross-legged on the floor with your spine erect.

3. Relax your neck by rotating it, first to the right and then to the left. Tense your shoulders up; then let them fall and relax.

4. Take several deep cleansing breaths and, as you fully exhale the last one, feel your tension leave.

5. Concentrate on a mantra (a prayer, chant, or hymn) or a monosyllabic word, such as OM.

6. Remain still for ten to fifteen minutes while attempting to control your thoughts, letting your spiritual nature nourish you.

7. Open your eyes, and come slowly back to conscious awareness. Take another deep breath, and feel yourself enveloped in the healing flow. Now you are ready to return to your outer world, feeling renewed and regenerated from the power within.

When you don't have time in your busy schedule to seek a secluded spot and practice meditation, there is an alternative discipline to call upon to access the same healing power. We call this exercise the practice of deep relaxation, as you can accomplish this on the job, in your kitchen, or while sitting in an airplane or bus. It only requires two minutes of your time.

Deep Relaxation

For deep relaxation, follow these five steps:

1. No particular space is needed for this practice, just yourself.

2. Lift your head up, stick out your chin, and tense your neck; then drop your head toward your chest thinking, "I relax my head and I release my mind from all tension."

3. Continue down your body in the same manner—neck, shoulders (tense, then relax); chest, arms, hands (tense, then relax); abdomen, hips, thighs (tense, then relax); and finally, legs, calves, ankles, and feet—releasing all parts of the body from tension.

4. Breathe quietly and rhythmically, feeling the healing energy flow throughout your body.

5. Now, mentally send healing to any part of your body that still feels tense, knowing that health and happiness are yours to claim.

PART II

CHAPTER IV:

THE SEVEN GODDESSES

ATHENA

The Female Communicator

Step I: Understanding Your Personality

The mythical Athena, the daughter and favorite child of Zeus, was the patron of the city of Athens. She was a fierce protector, sometimes manly, but also generous to the people. She was believed to embody wisdom, reason, and intelligence—and was often referred to as the warrior/goddess.

ᐭ

The Creative Wellness Athena is a woman of strong character who loves to express herself through various communications media. She desires to be in the limelight and, despite her strong constitution, she can break down under stress when she disregards her physical and emotional needs.

If you have been typed an Athena, you are a strong, outgoing, and competitive woman. You have a great need to express independence in your lifestyle. You usually want to be recognized and thrive on being considered a forerunner in your chosen profession. You are of above average intelligence and most likely have a strong educational background as well. However, you do not like details and prefer to delegate responsibilities to others. Socially, you like to be the knowledgeable authority on who's who, what's what, and what's new on the horizon. You like to be recognized by your peers for your superior judgment, excellent taste, and astuteness in understanding current events.

You are the sophisticated lady of the times, the trendsetter. Thriving on competition, you love to involve yourself in endeavors that may lead to personal stardom and that involve a certain amount of risk. When you spend your time on challenging and rewarding activities rather than on boring ones that leave you unrecognized, you are happy and can handle an active lifestyle well.

The contemporary women who fit the archetype of the Athena goddesses, even though not personally tested, are Barbara Walters, Diane Sawyer, Nancy Reagan, and Sharon Stone. These dynamic women exhibit the characters of strength, social graces, and above-average intelligence.

Most of Athena's stresses develop when people in authority don't appreciate them for being the capable women they are. They despise any form of criticism or rejection, especially when unwarranted. This over-reaction to outside opinions began in childhood, when Athena was not understood or allowed to express her inner truths. This was usually caused by an overly dominant parent. When criticized, the Athena woman tends to choke on or hold back her feelings, and can lash out unexpectedly at those who have upset her. While this anger may hurt others, it can often be internalized and harm Athena's health.

Your Creative Wellness challenge—and as an Athena, you love challenges—is to create a lifestyle, including a career, that gives you personal freedom of expression and choice. You need to protect yourself from frustrations that restrict or repress your uniqueness. One of your exceptional qualities is your good taste, so you need to surround yourself with beauty and fine things, but be careful not to become materially extravagant. This can cause you stress.

Your physical constitution, which is usually better than that of the average woman, will help you enjoy a full and active life. Unfortunately, after you turn forty, when natural hormonal changes occur in your body, you can age very quickly unless you follow a healthy regimen: plenty of fresh air and exercise, a high-protein, low-fat diet, and hobbies and activities that stimulate your intelligence and your requirement for self-expression.

Since your innate vulnerability is centered in your thyroid gland, and this weakness is heightened over the years from stress caused by your internal struggle with authority, the thyroid loses its ability to regulate your metabolism and cellular rejuvenation. To offset this body abuse, you need only become sensitive to your needs. You require relaxation and play. Express your emotions by acquiring relationships with people you can be yourself with, and allow yourself spontaneity. This will release the wonderful attributes that make you one of the looked-up-to and admired goddesses. You can be the star in any circumstance. You need only use your charm, not your sword, to win your audience over.

STRENGTHS AND WEAKNESSES

As an Athena, you embody these strengths:

- ✧ A trendsetter disposition
- ✧ Natural leadership abilities
- ✧ Keen intellect
- ✧ Excellent communication skills
- ✧ Innate good taste
- ✧ Love of competition
- ✧ A drive for success

Athena's inherent weaknesses are:

- ✧ Repressed emotions, a result of being stifled as a child
- ✧ An overly defensive nature
- ✧ Quickness to temper when personal freedom is threatened
- ✧ Difficulty dealing with authority figures, particularly women
- ✧ Escapism through material extravagances and pleasures
- ✧ A disregard for others' sensitivities
- ✧ An inability to handle criticism well

Step II: Reprogramming Your Psyche

ATHENA'S AFFIRMATION

I accept responsibility
For my past misdirected emotions,
Which have caused me to have

An imbalance in my psyche.
I now pledge to change
This detrimental habit
So I can live in a more balanced manner —
Spirit, mind and body as One.
Knowing that I can become
A true humanitarian, Sensitive to myself
And to the needs of others
I make this commitment now
And I project this awareness
Into my everyday lifestyle.

INCENSE

Lavender, gardenia, lemon, sandalwood, and strawberry

CANDLES

Red: for emotional expression
Green: for healing childhood traumas
White: for developing higher awareness

Step III: Creating Healthy Nutrition

Refer to Chapter VI, Pages 209 – 228.

Step IV: Color Support in the Wardrobe

ATHENA'S PALETTE COLORS

Supporting Colors

Balancers	Securers	Inspirers	Protectors
Dark brown	Burgundy	Shrimp	Charcoal
Sienna brown	Melon	Peach	Silver
Gold	Honey	Champagne	Ginger
Evergreen	Cream	Celery	Pumpkin
Emerald green	Apple green	Mint	Sunshine yellow
Navy	Leaf green	Eggshell blue	Wheat
Plum	Bright blue	Mauve	Turquoise

Avoidance Colors

Athena needs to avoid all bright reds in her wardrobe whenever possible. Even though she likes red and may think that she feels good in it, most reds overly stimulate her thyroid/adrenal relay circuitry, making her nervous and aggressively defensive. These reactions cause her to lose her sensitivity to herself, and often will create physical and emotional blowouts.

Step V: Gem and Stone Strengthening

WELLNESS SUPPORT STONES FOR ATHENA

For the Physical Body

- Indian agate – supports energy levels
- Petrified wood or picture agate – stabilizes hormonal function

- Jasper (all colors except red) – increases energy levels
- Garnet – regulates metabolism

For the Emotional System

- Mother-of-pearl – fosters nurturing qualities
- Mexican lace agate – prevents emotional disappointment
- Moonstone – encourages self-love
- Amber – protects against stress

For Spiritual and Mental Awareness

- Blue lace agate – fosters mental relaxation
- Lapis lazuli – expands mental faculties
- Malachite – unites reasoning and intuition
- Tiger's eye – gives clear discernment

Step VI: Scents, Herbal Elixirs, and Oils

ATHENA'S SCENTS, ELIXIRS, AND OILS

Athena's scents calm her nervous system; her elixirs help rejuvenate her skin, and her oils support her overall youthfulness.

Scents	Elixirs	Oils
Lavender	Aloe	Almond
Gardenia	Cucumber	Apricot/Peach
Lemon	Mint	Jojoba
Sandalwood	Avocado	Vitamine E
Strawberry	Lanolin	Lemon

Step VII: *Hobbies and Interests*

ATHENA'S PERSONALITY KEY

Athena loves to shine. She is both competitive and image conscious and so should consider activities that require skill and competition. At the same time, she should choose something that allows her to prove herself a star.

Outdoor

- ✧ Deep-sea fishing
- ✧ Playing tennis
- ✧ Sailing and white-water rafting
- ✧ Watching outdoor sports
- ✧ Snow and water skiing
- ✧ Traveling on short trips
- ✧ Participating in equestrian sports

Indoor

- ✧ Serving as community arts patron
- ✧ Attending social events like parties and conventions
- ✧ Doing aerobics or gymnastics
- ✧ Attending fashion shows
- ✧ Reading about current events
- ✧ Going to plays and movies
- ✧ Creating original designs in fashion and makeup

Step VIII: Exercises for Glandular Improvement

Athena's Exercise Routine

These exercises are meant to augment, not replace, your regular exercise routine. For further information , see the Recommended Reading section at the end of this book.

Athena's exercises have been divided into four categories: glandular strengthening, overall toning, relaxation, and rejuvenation to prevent premature aging and improve thyroid function.

1. Glandular strengthening: Head, neck, and shoulder rolls (for five minutes).

2. Overall toning: Warm-ups with aerobic jog in place; then, upper torso stretches, push-ups and modified sit-ups (for ten minutes).

3. Relaxation: Yoga shoulder stand pose (see Figure 5), followed by neck stretching or Yoga fish pose (for two to five minutes).

4. Rejuvenation: Deep relaxation (see Step X) and creative visualization to release tension and stimulate healing flow throughout the body. Relaxation techniques to be practiced in a prone position (for ten minutes).

Figure 5 • Shoulder Stand Pose

Step IX: Divine Relationships

ATHENA'S MALE COMPATIBILITY CHART

	EXCELLENT	VERY GOOD	GOOD	FAIR	POOR
ROMANCE	EROS	BACCHUS	NEPTUNE	APOLLO MERCURY ATLAS	HERMES
FRIENDSHIP		BACCHUS EROS	APOLLO NEPTUNE	ATLAS MERCURY	HERMES
WORK		BACCHUS	APOLLO EROS NEPTUNE	ATLAS HERMES MERCURY	

You, as an Athena, find the god Eros the most appealing of men, but are also attracted to Bacchus, Neptune, and Apollo. Their personalities reflect back to you what you would most like to enhance within yourself – youthfulness, wisdom, and sensitivity. For the pancreas type gods, you need to have a little more understanding and patience, as these men are often your professional coworkers. Leave the job behind, and go play with the men you love the most, and let your heart find your kindred soul, as he is a god wanting a goddess too.

Athena, you choose your female friends from those who support your interests in work, leisure time, and hard play. Skilled, intelligent women challenge you rather than threaten, unless you are both after the same professional position or romantic interlude. Athena, Aphrodite, and Diana nicely flow with you in most situations, but women focused on domesticity are not always to your liking, as you prefer friends who, like yourself, cherish their personal freedom. You create long-term friendships only where there is mutual respect and trust; all other relationships are usually short-lived.

Step X: The Inner Power – Meditation

Meditation Exercise

To meditate you should follow these seven basic steps:

1. Find a quiet area or corner of a room where you will not be disturbed. Near you, place a favorite religious or spiritual object, such as a statue, a crystal, or a mandala.

2. Sit on a straight-backed chair with your feet firmly planted on the floor, or sit cross-legged on the floor with your spine erect.

3. Relax your neck by rotating it, first to the right and then to the left. Tense your shoulders up; then let them fall and relax.

4. Take several deep cleansing breaths and, as you fully exhale the last one, you feel your tension leave.

5. Concentrate on a mantra (a prayer, chant, or hymn) or a monosyllabic word, such as OM.

6. Remain still for ten to fifteen minutes while attempting to control your thoughts, letting your spiritual nature nourish you.

7. Open your eyes, and come slowly back to conscious awareness. Take another deep breath, and feel yourself enveloped in the healing flow. Now you are ready to return to your outer world, feeling renewed and regenerated from the power within.

Deep Relaxation

For deep relaxation, follow these five steps:

1. No particular space is needed for this practice, just yourself.

2. Lift your head up, stick out your chin and tense your neck; then drop your head toward your chest thinking, "I relax my head and I release my mind from all tension."

3. Continue down your body in the same manner – neck, shoulders (tense, then relax); chest, arms, hands (tense, then relax); abdomen, hips, thighs (tense, then relax); and finally, legs, calves, ankles, and feet – releasing all parts of the body from tension.

4. Breathe quietly and rhythmically, feeling the healing energy flow throughout your body.

5. Now, mentally send healing to any part of your body that still feels tense, knowing that health and happiness are yours to claim.

ARTEMIS

The Lady Executive

Step I: Understanding Your Personality

The mythical Artemis, Apollo's twin sister and the daughter of Zeus and Leto, was the goddess of the moon and the protectress of youth. She was an earth woman and loved the mountains and forests. Her power was often magical, and she was known to be both the nurturer and the aggressor.

The Creative Wellness Artemis is an executive lady who can manage corporate and family affairs equally well. A difficulty understanding her emotional needs is her main stumbling block to success.

If you have been identified as an Artemis personality, you are a modern executive woman—an intelligent, self-motivated high-achiever. You love your independence and thrive on originality and ingenuity. These traits, along with your natural leadership abilities, often elevate you to top management roles in your profession.

Unfortunately, these traits can also make your peers and subordinates resentful and jealous of your capabilities. To them you may seem overbearing and aggressive. But those who see you this way and criticize you as an opportunist are usually the same people who would like to be in your position but lack the drive and stamina to succeed as you do. Their misguided reactions may lead you to question your self-worth.

Beneath the surface you are very sensitive, at times uncertain of the great potential you actually have. These feelings of sensitivity and uncertainty date from your childhood, when you felt unloved. As a child, you compensated for a lack of affection by concentrating on your mental capabilities. However, while developing your mind, you repressed certain emotional needs and built a shell around yourself, growing to depend less on your intuition and true feelings and more on your practical skills. Your drive to succeed may have given the appearance that you disregarded another's feelings, especially during your early womanhood years.

The contemporary Artemis of today can be imaged in the personalities of Hillary Rodham Clinton, Sandra Day O'Connor, Oprah Winfrey, and Jaclyn Smith—great women of high character and fame.

Just as your emotional vulnerabilities are masked from most people, your physical weaknesses are not always clear to you. Artemis types have a tendency to develop thyroid problems, and you may have developed symptoms of these between your mid-teens and your early thirties but failed to recognize them. Typical symptoms are weight irregularity (excessive gain or loss), periods of depression and/or anxiety, and frequent mood swings. You may even suffer from hyper- or hypothyroidism, in which case you should see a physician once you recognize these symptoms.

However, as a self-motivated Artemis, chances are good that you have already recognized your physical vulnerabilities and either prevented serious thyroid problems from developing or sought ways to deter them from interfering with good health. By ensuring your personal security, you have provided yourself the emotional and physical supports necessary to relieve tension and excessive worry.

Your Creative Wellness challenge, as with Athena, is to create a balanced lifestyle. Take time for simple self-improvement steps that guarantee good health, such as proper nutrition, daily exercise, and other natural supports that help you cope with a high-stress environment. If you do not begin to pay attention to your physical well-being and your inner spiritual power, you can become a candidate for a life-threatening illness.

Self-discovery is your path to good health. You are the goddess with magical powers to make your dreams come true. Once you put your heart into personal transformation, no challenge is too great for you. You can have it all: a superb career, good relationships with a lover or mate, happy motherhood, and loads of interesting outside activities. You can become a model for others: the balanced woman, the leader in the community, and the modern executive involved in global transformation.

STRENGTHS AND WEAKNESSES

You are now typed as Artemis, the mythological goddess who embodies these strengths:

- ✧ Natural leadership abilities
- ✧ Self-motivated and success-oriented
- ✧ A keen sense of logic
- ✧ Capability to complete self-initiated tasks
- ✧ Thrive on responsibility
- ✧ An appreciation of originality
- ✧ A natural transformer and change-agent

Artemis' inherent weaknesses are:

- ✧ Feelings of abandonment from childhood
- ✧ Fear of admitting to emotional sensitivity
- ✧ Overly aggressive mannerisms
- ✧ Prideful and manipulative tendencies
- ✧ A disposition to disregard another's feelings
- ✧ An obsessive drive to overwork
- ✧ Insensitivity to her own physical requirements

Step II: Reprogramming Your Psyche

ARTEMIS' AFFIRMATION

I accept myself as having
Certain inbred insecurities
That have led me to make wrong choices
Concerning my needs
For love, health, and balance.
In acknowledging these weaknesses,
I choose to change myself
So that I might realize
A more balanced lifestyle.
I affirm to bring health
And happiness to myself
With new opportunities to share
This awareness with others.

INCENSE

Honeysuckle, lily of the valley, sandalwood, patchouli,
and potpourri or spices

CANDLES

Dark red: for emotional sensitivity
Orange: for faith in self
White: for trusting intuitive insights

Step III: Creating Healthy Nutrition

Refer to Chapter VI, Pages 209 – 228.

Step IV: Color Support in the Wardrobe

ARTEMIS' PALETTE COLORS

Supporting Colors

Balancers	Securers	Inspirers	Protectors
Dark brown	Chinese red	Rose beige	Charcoal gray
Saddle brown	Apricot	Peach	Rust
Cream	Honey	Champagne	Pumpkin
Emerald green	Apple green	Celery	Gold
Evergreen	Leaf green	Mint	Lemon yellow
Navy blue	Bright blue	Sky blue	Wheat
Silver	Stone gray	Mauve	Turquoise

Avoidance Colors

Artemis needs to avoid all deep reds, especially the maroons, wines, and deep magentas, since she has an inherent thyroid weakness, and these colors irritate its ability to regulate metabolism. When she wears dark reds, she is prone to mood swings, irritability, and nervousness.

ᖇ

Step V: Gem and Stone Strengthening

WELLNESS SUPPORT STONES FOR ARTEMIS

For the Physical Body

- Carnelian – maintains pancreatic function
- Bloodstone – improves circulation
- Indian agate – supports energy levels
- Garnet – regulates metabolism

For the Emotional System

- Mexican lace agate – fosters happiness
- Moonstone – encourages self-love
- Black onyx – aids emotional protection
- Moss agate – provides emotional security

For Spiritual and Mental Awareness

- Blue lace agate – fosters mental relaxation
- Malachite – unites reasoning and intuition
- Lapis lazuli – expands mental faculties
- Crystals – heighten inner awareness

Step VI: Scents, Herbal Elixirs, and Oils

ARTEMIS' SCENTS, ELIXIRS, AND OILS

Artemis' scents help to lift her spirits; her elixirs aid overall self-improvement, and her oils rejuvenate her body.

Scents	Elixirs	Oils
Honeysuckle	Aloe	Jojoba
Lily of the valley	Herbal Mixtures	Christmas Pine
Sandalwood	Chamomile	Lemon/Lime
Patchouli	Peach	Lavender
Potpourri or Spice	Milk and Honey	Castor

Step VII: Hobbies and Interests

ARTEMIS' PERSONALITY KEY

Artemis likes to be in control and enjoys activities best if they give her a chance to exert that control. She should consider activities and hobbies that are challenging and require skill.

Outdoor

- ✧ Target shooting – skeet or archery
- ✧ Spelunking and rappelling
- ✧ Golfing

Outdoor *(continued)*

- ✧ Miniature golfing
- ✧ Jogging
- ✧ Deep-sea fishing
- ✧ Traveling abroad (first class)

Indoor

- ✧ Attending symphonies and operas
- ✧ Participating in civic activities
- ✧ Painting with oils and watercolors
- ✧ Doing crossword and jigsaw puzzles
- ✧ Playing video and computer games
- ✧ Playing bridge and Trivial Pursuit
- ✧ Participating in health clubs

Step VIII: Exercises for Glandular Improvement

Artemis' Exercise Routines

These exercises are meant to augment, not replace, your regular exercise routine. For further information , see the Recommended Reading section at the end of this book.

Artemis' exercises have been divided into four categories: warm-ups, toning exercises, rejuvenation, and relaxation for improving metabolism and thyroid function.

1. Warm-ups: Stretching the spine; head, neck, and shoulder rolls (see Figure 6); rocking the hips; and jumping-jacks (for five minutes).

2. Toning Exercises: Arm push-offs, or two-lb. weight lifting, waist bends, leg raises, and modified sit-ups (for ten minutes).

3. Rejuvenation: Trampoline bouncing, or aerobic step-dancing (for five to ten minutes).

4. Relaxation: Guided meditation in prone position with music or tape (for ten minutes).

Figure 6 • Head, Neck, and Shoulder Rolls

Step IX: Divine Relationships

ARTEMIS' MALE COMPATIBILITY CHART

	EXCELLENT	VERY GOOD	GOOD	FAIR	POOR
ROMANCE	ATLAS	HERMES	EROS	BACCHUS APOLLO MERCURY	NEPTUNE
FRIENDSHIP		ATLAS HERMES	EROS MERCURY	APOLLO BACCHUS NEPTUNE	
WORK		ATLAS HERMES EROS	APOLLO MERCURY	BACCHUS	NEPTUNE

You, as an Artemis, love and appreciate the pancreas type personalities, especially the Atlas, for he holds up the world for you. Simultaneously, these men appreciate your independence and leadership abilities, so they do not threaten your natural executive talents.

At times, you have difficulty with the overly independent archetypal gods, because cooperation can become a contest of wills, rather than a comfortable interaction, causing you stress. With these men, show more charity, and they will give back to you all the honor and respect you deserve.

Artemis, you choose as female friends those you could consider sisters in both work and play. However, these women should never consider themselves equal partners to you, since most of you believe "intimacy breeds contempt." Minerva, Aphrodite, Diana, and Athena, in that order, are your potentially divine all-around female companions. The adrenal types are sometimes too emotional for your liking, as you prefer to keep things under your control. If you are sensitive to yourself and another, you can easily create long, enduring friendships that are well remembered over the years.

Step X: The Inner Power – Meditation

Mediation Exercise

To meditate you should follow these seven basic steps:

1. Find a quiet area or corner of a room where you will not be disturbed. Near you, place a favorite religious or spiritual object, such as a statue, a crystal, or a mandala.

2. Sit on a straight-backed chair with your feet firmly planted on the floor, or sit cross-legged on the floor with your spine erect.

3. Relax your neck by rotating it, first to the right and then to the left. Tense your shoulders up; then let them fall and relax.

4. Take several deep cleansing breaths and, as you fully exhale the last one, you feel your tension leave.

5. Concentrate on a mantra (a prayer, chant, or hymn) or a monosyllabic word, such as OM.

6. Remain still for ten to fifteen minutes while attempting to control your thoughts, letting your spiritual nature nourish you.

7. Open your eyes, and come slowly back to conscious awareness. Take another deep breath, and feel yourself enveloped in the healing flow. Now you are ready to return to your outer world, feeling renewed and regenerated from the power within.

Deep Relaxation

For deep relaxation, follow these five steps:

1. No particular space is needed for this practice, just yourself.

2. Lift your head up, stick out your chin and tense your neck; then drop your head toward your chest thinking, "I relax my head, and I release my mind from all tension."

3. Continue down your body in the same manner—neck, shoulders (tense, then relax); chest, arms, hands (tense, then relax); abdomen, hips, thighs (tense, then relax); and finally, legs, calves, ankles, and feet—releasing all parts of the body from tension.

4. Breathe quietly and rhythmically, feeling the healing energy flow throughout your body.

5. Now, mentally send healing to any part of your body that still feels tense, knowing that health and happiness are yours to claim.

IRIS

The Natural Intuitive

Step I: Understanding Your Personality

The mythical Iris, goddess of the rainbow, lived in Olympus and delivered messages from the gods to men. Along with Hermes, she intervened to protect Greek heroes from monsters they encountered on their travels. She had a benevolent nature but was not afraid to speak the truth, no matter how unpleasant to the receiver.

The Creative Wellness Iris is an organizational humanitarian who loves involvement with others, but her suppressed sensitivity can be her physical and emotional undoing.

If your test shows you to be an Iris, you would no doubt like your personality spelled out clearly for you, since you feel that few people see you as you really are. This is particularly true because you tend to hide your feelings from others. Since you appear secure and unruffled most of the time, most people don't realize how sensitive you truly are. You are philosophical and idealistic and can often intuit what is not immediately apparent to another. When you trust your feelings, you are the natural psychic, and your intuition will never let you down.

Your particular persona is imaged by many of the leading psychics or seeresses of today, such as Jeanne Dixon, Linda Goodman, and Patricia Aburdene. These women are all humanitarian futurists profiling individual intuitive gifts.

Unfortunately, this sensitive aspect of your personality can affect your health adversely because you have a tendency to absorb the vibrations of others, particularly their stresses. You are vulnerable to any inherent weakness in your pituitary-adrenal-ovarian reflex circuitry. When under stress, you can suffer from "combat fatigue," which is a weakening condition of your autoimmune system. Negative stress overtaxes the pituitary (the master gland of your body), exhausts your adrenals, and depletes your sexual energy and libido. When low in energy, you have a habit of procrastination, defending your actions by excuses and imaginary reasons for not becoming involved. This overdefensiveness can make you susceptible to physical ills, such as hypertension, allergies, viruses, colds, and eventually lung and heart problems, because of inner conflict over what you want to do and what you feel you're capable of doing.

The sensitive Iris always has a calm facade. However, at times she hides her frustrations and resentfulness behind this mask, allowing the pressure to build so much that she can reach a boiling point, where she either blows or escapes into her own world. This escapist tendency started at an early age when her sensitivities were not understood by one or both of her parents. As a result today, she still becomes irritated at people who ignore her feelings or fail to reward her for her contributions.

The Creative Wellness Plan can be particularly helpful to you , an Iris, since, more than any other goddess, you need to learn how to nurture yourself. To be the humanitarian that you are by nature and help others, you must first help yourself. You need to find creative ways to express your emotions and therapeutic means to care for your body, such as a monthly massage, a facial, and frequent visits to the chiropractor to balance your energies. Since Iris types generally love history, you would probably benefit from travel, visiting museums, historical sites, archaeological digs, and antique shows. You love to read and would find creative expression in inspirational writing and diary keeping.

Nurturing yourself and trying to understand your emotions can also help you develop your natural psychic gifts. To be a good intuitive, you must have internal clarity and strength of mind and body to serve the needs of others. Once liberated from early life traumas, you'll be free to pursue the mysteries of life and find yourself capable of helping the world as only a messenger of the gods can.

STRENGTHS AND WEAKNESSES

You are now typed as Iris, the mythological goddess who embodies these strengths:

- ✧ Creative imagination
- ✧ Innate psychic ability
- ✧ Philanthropic inclinations
- ✧ A natural love of tradition and culture
- ✧ Emotional independence and self-containment
- ✧ Keen insight into others
- ✧ A talent for peacemaking and arbitration

Iris' inherent weaknesses are:

- ✧ Preoccupation with one's own past traumas early in life
- ✧ Escapist tendencies
- ✧ Oversensitivity to environment
- ✧ A readiness to despair when goals are not being met
- ✧ Predisposed to become resentful
- ✧ A tendency to procrastinate
- ✧ Failure to nurture self and attend to personal needs

Step II: Reprogramming Your Psyche

IRIS' AFFIRMATION

I acknowledge that in my past
I have allowed my repressed sensitivity
To traumatize me.
Therefore I choose now
To alter these past patterns
By cultivating healthy habits,
And changing my present lifestyle.
In affirming this desire,
I bring myself one step closer
To personal realization of my
Spirit, mind, and body as one.

INCENSE

Rose, jasmine, orange blossom, patchouli, and musk

CANDLES

Dark blue: for self-responsibility
Green: for healing over sensitivity
Violet: for developing spiritual gifts

Step III: Creating Healthy Nutrition

Refer to Chapter VII, Pages 247 – 265.

Step IV: Color Support in the Wardrobe

IRIS' PALETTE COLORS

Supporting Colors

Balancers	Securers	Inspirers	Protectors
Saddle brown	Crimson red	Rose beige	Burgundy
Ginger	Shrimp	Peach	French gray
Wheat	Oyster	Tan	Honey
Gold	Sunshine yellow	Champagne	Teal
Evergreen	Turquoise	Mint	Navy blue
Midnight blue	Wedgewood blue	Eggshell blue	Grape
Purple	Violet	Lilac	Magenta

Avoidance Colors

Iris needs to avoid all bright greens, since these colors do not support her natural immunity in a stressful environment. When wearing the Kelly and shamrock greens, she feels secure on the emotional level, but is left physically defenseless.

Step V: Gem and Stone Strengthening

WELLNESS SUPPORT STONES FOR IRIS

For the Physical Body

- Bloodstone – improves circulation
- Amber – protects the adrenal system
- Coral (all colors) – stimulates hormonal production
- Red moss agate, red jasper, or plume agate – increases libido

For the Emotional System

- Rhodochrosite – restores depleted emotions
- Moonstone – encourages self-understanding
- Pearl – promotes self-nurturing
- Shells and fossils – reduces nervous tension

For Spiritual and Mental Awareness

- Tiger's eye or falcon's eye – gives clear insight
- Amethyst – increases intuition
- Jade (all colors) – expands practicality
- Tourmaline – fosters inner peace

Step VI: Scents, Herbal Elixirs, and Oils

IRIS' SCENTS, ELIXIRS, AND OILS

Iris' scents give added protection to her sensitivity, her elixirs help maintain a youthful appearance, and her oils restore and rejuvenate her energy.

Scents	Elixirs	Oils
Rose	Rose Water & Glycerine	Almond
Jasmine	Avocado	Apricot Kernel
Orange blossom	Cocoa Butter	Eucalyptus
Patchouli	Aloe	Lavender
Musk	Oatmeal	Vitamin E

Step VII: Hobbies and Interests

IRIS' PERSONALITY KEY

Iris loves history and humanitarian activities. She should consider noncompetitive hobbies and sports, as well as humanitarian and preservation-oriented activities.

Outdoor

- ✧ Camping
- ✧ Hiking or taking long walks
- ✧ Gardening
- ✧ Going on wilderness excursions and retreats
- ✧ Hunting rocks or artifacts
- ✧ Touring, at home or abroad
- ✧ Bay fishing – crabbing and clamming

Indoor

- ✧ Visiting museums and restoration projects
- ✧ Oil painting and making ceramics
- ✧ Ballroom dancing
- ✧ Attending antiques shows and flea markets
- ✧ Doing body-design exercises
- ✧ Reading historical and romantic novels
- ✧ Helping in community service organizations

Step VIII: Exercises for Glandular Improvement

Iris' Exercise Routines

These exercises are meant to augment, not replace, your regular exercise routine. For further information, see the Recommended Reading section at the end of this book.

Iris' exercises have been divided into three categories: warm-ups, toning exercises, and deep relaxation, which should be followed by an outdoor exercise for improved circulation, such as a brisk walk, a swim, or a dance class.

1. For Warm-ups: Stretching the spine, loosening upper torso by arm raises, hip swings, and knee bends (for ten minutes).

2. Toning exercises: Hip and pelvic rolls, modified sit-ups, waist bends, and Yoga kneeling pose (see Figure 7) (for ten minutes).

3. Deep relaxation: From a seated position—spine straight, hands in lap—relax body, starting with head and descending to feet to release tension. Breathe rhythmically to stimulate healing energy (for five to ten minutes).

Figure 7 • Yoga Kneeling Pose

Step IX: Divine Relationships

IRIS' MALE COMPATIBILITY CHART

	EXCELLENT	VERY GOOD	GOOD	FAIR	POOR
ROMANCE	EROS	BACCHUS NEPTUNE	ATLAS	APOLLO MERCURY	HERMES
FRIENDSHIP		BACCHUS EROS NEPTUNE	APOLLO ATLAS MERCURY	HERMES	
WORK		BACCHUS EROS MERCURY NEPTUNE	APOLLO ATLAS	HERMES	

ᘉ

You, as an Iris, love sensitive men. You are most attracted to an Eros, a Bacchus, and a Neptune in romance and friendship. Mercury stimulates your mind, but Eros and Bacchus your heart.

The male-oriented gods, or those with excessive needs, are not to your liking, as you prefer a noncompetitive relationship at home, as well as in the workplace. For a healthy lifestyle, your compatible partners must appreciate you, enjoy you, and show you concern, for you are the goddess of the rainbow, the messenger of sunshine.

Iris, you have many female friends and coworkers to choose from among the goddesses, for you are naturally sensitive to another's need. You admire other Irises, flow well with Athenas, create well with Venuses, and appreciate Aphrodites and Minervas. So long as your friends truly honor your worth and recognize your contributions to the relationship, they are guaranteed to have a loyal supporter in you. However, women who constantly focus attention on their own requirements seldom can count themselves long-term best friends. Enough is enough, and when you see into the heart of the matter, the situation clears or the relationship is over.

Step X: The Inner Power—Meditation

Meditation Exercise

To meditate you should follow these seven basic steps:

1. Find a quiet area or corner of a room where you will not be disturbed. Near you, place a favorite religious or spiritual object, such as a statue, a crystal, or a mandala.

2. Sit on a straight-backed chair with your feet firmly planted on the floor, or sit cross-legged on the floor with your spine erect.

3. Relax your neck by rotating it, first to the right and then to the left. Tense your shoulders up; then let them fall and relax.

4. Take several deep cleansing breaths and, as you fully exhale the last one, you feel your tension leave.

5. Concentrate on a mantra (a prayer, chant, or hymn) or a monosyllabic word, such as OM.

6. Remain still for ten to fifteen minutes while attempting to control your thoughts, letting your spiritual nature nourish you.

7. Open your eyes, and come slowly back to conscious awareness. Take another deep breath, and feel yourself enveloped in the healing flow. Now you are ready to return to your outer world, feeling renewed and regenerated from the power within.

Deep Relaxation

For deep relaxation, follow these five steps:

1. No particular space is needed for this practice, just yourself.

2. Lift your head up, stick out your chin and tense your neck; then drop your head toward your chest thinking, "I relax my head and I release my mind from all tension."

3. Continue down your body in the same manner—neck, shoulders (tense, then relax); chest, arms, hands (tense, then relax); abdomen, hips, thighs (tense, then relax); and finally, legs, calves, ankles, and feet—releasing all parts of the body from tension.

4. Breathe quietly and rhythmically, feeling the healing energy flow throughout your body.

5. Now, mentally send healing to any part of your body that still feels tense, knowing that health and happiness are yours to claim.

VENUS

Ms. Innovative Entrepreneur

Step I: Understanding Your Personality

The mythical Venus, goddess of love, beguiled both men and gods with her irresistible beauty and laughter. Romans honored her as the protectress of gardens and the embodiment of the creative forces of life. The planet Venus is named for her.

The Creative Wellness Venus personifies femininity at work and at home. She can meet all creative challenges, but self-victimization can undermine her health and stamina.

If you have been tested as a Venus, you are naturally creative and resourceful. You have a generous and charismatic nature. However, because of your childlike innocence, beauty, and physical frailty, you may find yourself easily victimized. This does not mean that you are a weak woman— rather the opposite. Under your guileless demeanor lies great inner strength. You are also philosophic and compassionate, for you seek to understand the meaning of life. You have the ability to access and solve problems quickly which gives the potential to be an independent achiever and entrepreneur. As a Venus, you also have a natural gift for conversation and love both entertaining and being entertained. You are steadfast in friendship, and like your archetypal namesake, you are what most people admire: a loving, confident woman who wins the heart of everyone she meets. Contemporary women who fit the Venus profile are Kathy Lee Gifford, Melanie Griffith, Connie Chung, and the great founder of the cosmetic company, Elizabeth Arden. These dynamic women personify beauty and independence.

Having a fear of rejection, you often assume the role of the victim. Some of the blame can probably be placed on rejection or emotional abuse, usually not physical abuse, from a father figure in early childhood. Not all the blame, Venus, as you have inherited certain physical frailties—more than any other goddess—that make you susceptible to stress-related illness. You are especially prone to traumas caused by major life changes; such as losing a partner, changing a job, moving to a new location, or even having a baby or getting married. When your reality is altered or threatened in any manner, your innate frailties can manifest themselves in female irregularities or other physical symptoms, including despondency or despair.

Your physical or emotional weaknesses are centered in your adrenal and sexual glands. Usually, these glands produce too few hormones and can leave you physically exhausted and emotionally temperamental. In time, the hormonal depletion can cause the body's autoimmune system to break down totally.

To maintain your sense of well-being, it is necessary that you, as a Venus, do not give away your power, nor permit another person or circumstance to control your life. You can use your natural resourcefulness to establish independence and maintain your control. Once you succeed, your playful and careful side will always surface, smiling at the world, for you have great resilience.

If you have been an abused woman, and if you are honest with yourself, you can start healing yourself immediately by being disciplined in the use of your Creative Wellness transformational tools, beginning with your Venus affirmation. Then, follow the program with the emotional-protective natural supports: vitamins, colors, gems, oils, and lotions. You will become once again a beautiful, playful female—the one you were destined to be, and men will admire and respect you, not abuse you.

To restore your energy, Venus, you can learn how to heal yourself with the power within. You can do this creatively. Since you have great inner strength, PMS and cramps will become a thing of the past, and menopause will be made easier in the future. You, the most creative of all goddesses can take command of your time, energy, and self-management, and be called the modern woman, sensitive, yet strong.

STRENGTHS AND WEAKNESSES

You are now typed as Venus, the mythological goddess who embodies these strengths:

- ✧ A fun-loving and playful nature
- ✧ Philosophic and compassionate virtues
- ✧ Steadfast in friendship
- ✧ Independent achiever
- ✧ Innate femininity
- ✧ Keen analytical abilities
- ✧ Great inner strength and faith

Venus' inherent weaknesses are:

- ✧ A tendency to repeat victimizing experiences
- ✧ Susceptibility to abuse and deception
- ✧ Anxiety about life's circumstances getting out of control
- ✧ Poor resistance to stress-induced disorders
- ✧ Proclivity to feelings of hopelessness and despair
- ✧ Inability to remain objective under stress
- ✧ Blaming others for mistakes of the past

Step II: Reprogramming Your Psyche

VENUS' AFFIRMATION

I acknowledge that in my past
I have allowed repeated victimization
To interfere with my physical well-being
And undermine my total balance.
I pledge now to release myself from this pattern
So I can live in health,
Creating new constructive habits.
This commitment will help me regain
The power within myself
To heal and transform my life,
Finding happiness in all that I am.

INCENSE

Rose, gardenia, lavender, lily of the valley, and musk

CANDLES

Red: for physical power
Rust: for emotional endurance
Pink: for self-love

Step III: Creating Healthy Nutrition

Refer to Chapter VII, Pages 247 – 265.

Step IV: Color Support in the Wardrobe

VENUS' PALETTE COLORS

Supporting Colors

Balancers	Securers	Inspirers	Protectors
Charcoal gray	Scarlet red	Pink	Cherry red
Saddle brown	Hot pink	Rose beige	Evergreen
Wheat	Gold	Champagne	Khaki
Cream	Citrus yellow	White	Turquoise
Navy blue	Teal	Mint	Royal Blue
Plum	Bright blue	Wedgwood blue	Lavender
Burgundy	Orchid	Lilac	Magenta

Avoidance Colors

Venus needs to avoid rusts, dark oranges, and red browns whenever possible. Although she may think that she feels secured and satisfied in these colors, she's left vulnerable to low libido, and prone to emotional victimization.

Step V: Gem and Stone Strengthening

WELLNESS SUPPORT STONES FOR VENUS

For the Physical Body

- Coral (especially red) – stimulates hormonal production
- Wood (petrified and agatized) – supports libido stamina

- Jasper (all colors) – increases physical energy
- Ivory, bone, fossil – strengthens body tone

For the Emotional System

- Tiger's eye – stabilizes the emotions
- Rhodochrosite – restores depleted emotions
- Amber – protects sensitive nature
- Pink quartz – builds self-esteem

For Spiritual and Mental Awareness

- Amethyst – enhances intuition
- Jade – promotes objectivity
- Opal – increases creativity and love
- Moonstone – fosters self-understanding

Step VI: Scents, Herbal Elixirs, and Oils

VENUS' SCENTS, ELIXIRS, AND OILS

Venus' scents help her to be in touch with her inner power, her elixirs aid her to maintain a youthful appearance, and her oils calm and relax her.

Scents	Elixirs	Oils
Rose	Rose Water & Glycerine	Almond
Gardenia	Lanolin	Apricot Kernel
Lavender	Clay or Mud	Musk
Lily of the valley	Milk & Honey	Rose
Musk	Cocoa Butter	Sage

Step VII: Hobbies and Interests

VENUS' PERSONALITY KEY

Venus loves to express her creativity in her personal appearance and in her home. Because of her weak constitution, she might consider activities that are emotionally satisfying but involve little physical competition.

Outdoor

- ✧ Gardening – vegetable and flower
- ✧ Going on short excursions
- ✧ Bicycling
- ✧ Watching sports
- ✧ Golfing
- ✧ Swimming
- ✧ Beach-combing

Indoor

- ✧ Attending comedies and musicals
- ✧ Ballet
- ✧ Playing board games – Scrabble, backgammon, checkers
- ✧ Interior decorating
- ✧ Reading romantic novels
- ✧ Taking photographs and studying photography
- ✧ Beautifying her body

Step VIII: Excercises for Glandular Improvement

Venus' Exercise Routines

These exercises are meant to augment, not replace, your regular exercise routine. For further information , see the Recommended Reading section at the end of this book.

Venus' exercises have been divided into three categories: warm-ups, toning exercises, and deep relaxation, which should be followed by an outdoor or indoor exercise for improved stamina, such as walking the dog, or bike-trail riding.

1. Warm-ups: Stretching the spine, arm raises, pelvic twists, knee lifts, and feet and ankle stretches (for ten minutes).

2. Toning exercises: Hip and pelvic lifts (see Figure 8), leg raises (one at a time), chest expanding exercises with small weights, and Yoga kneeling pose (for ten minutes).

3. Deep relaxation: From a seated position—spine straight, hands in lap, relax body with guided imagery from tape meditations. Allow healing flow to descend from head to toe (for five to ten minutes).

Figure 8 • Hip and Pelvic Lifts

Step IX: Divine Relationships

VENUS' MALE COMPATIBILITY CHART

	EXCELLENT	VERY GOOD	GOOD	FAIR	POOR
ROMANCE	APOLLO	EROS NEPTUNE	ATLAS BACCHUS	HERMES MERCURY	
FRIENDSHIP		APOLLO BACCHUS EROS	ATLAS NEPTUNE	HERMES MERCURY	
WORK		APOLLO BACCHUS NEPTUNE	ATLAS EROS HERMES		MERCURY

You, as a Venus, are very appealing to the opposite sex, and, sometimes to your own detriment, you don't always recognize which gods are best for you in relationships. Men who have inherent sensitive natures will love and respect yours, and you can bring out the best in them, if you don't turn over all your power.

Since Mercury and Hermes like conventional women, they threaten your need for independence. So, love them from afar, but do not create emotional entanglements with them, or you may be like the statue without arms.

Venus, you tend to choose your true friends selectively from the goddesses who, like yourself, have similar traits in their personality typing. You admire sensitivity and can count worthy Irises, liberated Aphrodites, evolved Athenas, and other creative Venuses on your friendship list. You shy away from either overbearing women who crave dominance, or co-dependent women who measure their worth, or lack of it, on another. You would rather go it alone, even with females, if you feared that sharing too much or being intimate with another could drain your power or threaten your existence.

Step X: The Inner Power – Meditation

Meditation Exercise

To meditate you should follow these seven basic steps:

1. Find a quiet area or corner of a room where you will not be disturbed. Near you, place a favorite religious or spiritual object, such as a statue, a crystal, or a mandala.

2. Sit on a straight-backed chair with your feet firmly planted on the floor, or sit cross-legged on the floor with your spine erect.

3. Relax your neck by rotating it, first to the right and then to the left. Tense your shoulders up; then let them fall and relax.

4. Take several deep cleansing breaths and, as you fully exhale the last one, you feel your tension leave.

5. Concentrate on a mantra (a prayer, chant, or hymn) or a monosyllabic word, such as OM.

6. Remain still for ten to fifteen minutes while attempting to control your thoughts, letting your spiritual nature nourish you.

7. Open your eyes, and come slowly back to conscious awareness. Take another deep breath, and feel yourself enveloped in the healing flow. Now you are ready to return to your outer world, feeling renewed and regenerated from the power within.

Deep Relaxation

For deep relaxation, follow these five steps:

1. No particular space is needed for this practice, just yourself.

2. Lift your head up, stick out your chin and tense your neck; then drop your head toward your chest thinking, "I relax my head and I release my mind from all tension."

3. Continue down your body in the same manner—neck, shoulders (tense, then relax); chest, arms, hands (tense, then relax); abdomen, hips, thighs (tense, then relax); and finally, legs, calves, ankles, and feet—releasing all parts of the body from tension.

4. Breathe quietly and rhythmically, feeling the healing energy flow throughout your body.

5. Now, mentally send healing to any part of your body that still feels tense, knowing that health and happiness are yours to claim.

MINERVA

The Community Nurturer

Step I: Understanding Your Personality

The mythical Minerva, the Roman counterpart of Athena, embodied caring, concern, and practicality—the goddess of the hearth. As protectress of civilized life, she could be warlike when defending her home. As patroness of handicrafts and skilled workers, she was a champion of community life.

The Creative Wellness Minerva is the community nurturer, handling challenges of modern day society with expertise and finesse. Unfortunately, this type of goddess doesn't always realize her great virtues, for at times she can feel unloved and unappreciated for her contributions to the community.

If you are one who has been identified as a Minerva, you are the Supermom of the goddesses. You have a basic need to nurture and at the same time be recognized for your creative abilities to support community life. You are very responsible, intelligent, and capable in all that you do, and a born teacher to others. Although you don't always believe that you are the foundation stone of the society, your civic-mindedness lends itself to the advancement of culture and education. Of all the goddesses, you alone are the mother's strength and can always manage to find creative ways to express your love for others, on the job and in the home.

You are capable of caring for everyone's needs, both small and large, whether by giving time to the American Red Cross, or by carpooling for work or children's sports. You have a great talent for attending to details and are organized in all that you do. Consequently, you usually choose a career where people involvement and details go hand in hand. You make a good teacher, healer, or community worker. You love the arts of living and usually are talented with your hands. Your interests at home include cooking, gardening, and animal husbandry.

∾

Recognized women who image your type of goddess are Barbara Bush, Betty White, Julia Childs, and Coretta Scott King. These ladies with their diversified interests are outstanding examples of the "Community Mother" personified.

Since the Creative Wellness Minerva often sees herself as duty bound and responsible for the home and family, she can sometimes be overly put upon, and though she may often feel used by others, she seldom verbalizes her pain. Rather, she can internalize it, making herself physically or emotionally ill.

You, as a Minerva, were not appreciated or praised enough as a child and this conditioning causes you feelings of dissatisfaction with yourself and your performance. You tend to judge yourself too harshly and consequently, may be too critical of others. Your basic requirement to be justly rewarded, not supplied by a parent when you were young, causes you to have an unconscious need to gratify yourself, particularly when frustrated. It may explain why you sometimes overindulge—perhaps by eating too much—to feel loved. You can rationalize a poor self-image by a statement like "Fat is beautiful," rather than face the fact that you need more self-caring, especially self-love. Or, you might have a large family, or raise and train animals, so as to substitute creatively your need for love returned.

Most Minervas form poor health habits at an early age, habits that lead to a myriad of pancreatic and digestive problems. However, once the problems are recognized and the detrimental habits altered, health is usually restored. Self-improvement disciplines, even though difficult for a Minerva, who struggles to persevere, can ensure better health and improved feelings of self-worth. You must dedicate yourself with your whole being to follow a health regime that supports you physically and emotionally.

To start a Creative Wellness Plan, you must start with a goal. Going on a diet with a support group, taking classes in your favorite subject, and setting time aside in your busy daily schedule for meditation are good beginnings. No excuses! By improving yourself, you will find more energy to be the great humanitarian nurturer that you are. You'll discover that others will recognize the changes that you are making in yourself and compliment you for your efforts. What a nice reward!

Minerva, never underestimate yourself; your grace, your innate sensitivity, your great generosity, and your tenacity can be a lesson to us all. Your spirit of giving and caring is honored from above and your humanitarian acts will never go unrewarded in the annals of time.

STRENGTHS AND WEAKNESSES

You are now typed as Minerva, the mythological goddess who embodies these strengths:

- ✧ Natural nurturing qualities
- ✧ A deep appreciation of nature
- ✧ Innate talent for teaching
- ✧ Competence in job performance
- ✧ Socially oriented and concerned citizen
- ✧ Proficient in the art and craft fields
- ✧ An ability to rejuvenate self

Minerva's inherent weaknesses are:

- ✧ A tendency to feel overburdened
- ✧ Repressed frustration with self and others
- ✧ Lack of self-esteem
- ✧ Overly critical of others
- ✧ Prone to feelings of guilt
- ✧ An inclination to become too involved in others' affairs
- ✧ A need to rationalize overindulgence

Step II: Reprogramming Your Psyche

MINERVA'S AFFIRMATION

I acknowledge that I have not understood
How to care
For myself as a total being.
Because of this misunderstanding,
I have had difficulties
Recognizing and loving myself.
Therefore, I now take constructive action
To learn to appreciate myself
So that my innate superior qualities
To heal and nurture others
May flow from me and return,
Bringing inner balance, peace, and happiness.

INCENSE

Frangipani, patchouli, honeysuckle, jasmine, and sage or wildflower

CANDLES

Orange: for self-confidence
Light blue: for creative insight
Pink: for self-love

Step III: Creating Healthy Nutrition

Refer to Chapter VIII, Pages 287 – 307.

Step IV: Color Support in the Wardrobe

MINERVA'S PALETTE COLORS

Supporting Colors

Balancers	Securers	Inspirers	Protectors
Saddle brown	Chinese red	Melon	Burgundy
Rust	Pumpkin	Apricot	Sienna brown
Gold	Honey	Oyster	Wheat
Apple green	Champagne	Celery	Sunshine yellow
Evergreen	Nile green	Mint	Emerald
Navy blue	Turquoise	Sky blue	Midnight blue
Black	Plum	Lavender	Pewter gray

Avoidance Colors

Minerva needs to avoid all pinks, from the palest of rose pink to hot pink. These nurturing colors give her a false sense of self-love and self-worth, as they intensify her urge to focus on others, neglecting her own needs. Also, when Minerva is drained, pinks will not restore her energy levels nor support pancreatic function.

Step V: Gem and Stone Strengthening

WELLNESS SUPPORT STONES FOR MINERVA

For the Physical Body

- Carnelian – stabilizes blood sugar levels
- Bloodstone and green Jasper – promote good circulation

For the Physical Body *(continued)*

- Indian agate – maintains physical stamina
- Jasper (all colors) – increases energy levels

For the Emotional System

- Blue lace agate – promotes tranquillity
- Sodalite – dispels a guilty conscience
- Moonstone – encourages self-love
- Tiger's eye – fosters control of the emotions

For Spiritual and Mental Awareness

- Jade (especially green) – increases wisdom
- Turquoise – gives inspiration
- Crystal – enhances healing abilities
- Pearl – fosters humanitarian love

Step VI: Scents, Herbal Elixirs, and Oils

MINERVA'S SCENTS, ELIXIRS, AND OILS

Minerva's scents help release her anxiousness and calm her, her elixirs aid her self-improvement, and her oils support her skin rejuvenation.

Scents	Elixirs	Oils
Frangipani	Comfrey	Almond
Patchouli	Cucumber	Jojoba
Honeysuckle	Aloe	Lemon/Lime
Jasmine	Oatmeal	Myrrh
Sage or Wildflower	Vitamins A & D	Peach/Apricot

Step VII: *Hobbies and Interests*

MINERVA'S PERSONALITY KEY

Minerva loves natural things and generally wants to share her knowledge. She should consider home and community activities, since these will make her feel emotionally secure and at peace with herself.

Outdoor

- ✧ Jogging short distances
- ✧ Roller skating and ice skating
- ✧ Camping
- ✧ Gardening and caring for the yard
- ✧ Canoeing and paddle boating
- ✧ Attending picnics and pool parties
- ✧ Attending fairs and other outdoor festivals

Indoor

- ✧ Square dancing and belly dancing
- ✧ Cooking – homestyle and gourmet
- ✧ Quilting, weaving, basket making
- ✧ Caring for indoor plants, terrariums, greenhouses
- ✧ Participating in fitness clubs
- ✧ Breeding domestic pets and attending pet shows
- ✧ Participating in community activities—PTA, arts and craft shows

Step VIII: Exercises for Glandular Improvement
Minerva's Exercise Routine

These exercises are meant to augment, not replace, your regular exercise routine. For further information, see the Recommended Reading section at the end of this book.

Minerva's exercises have been divided into four categories: warm-ups, tummy tighteners, spinal flexors, and relaxation for improved digestion and elimination. You, a Minerva, enjoy being supported during an exercise regime, so go to the health club, to an aerobic dance class, or participate in a T'ai Chi or Yoga class, as these will enhance your sense of well-being.

1. Warm-ups: At home, bend and stretch exercises upon arising (for five minutes).

2. Tummy tighteners: Modified sit-ups, knee hugs (see Figure 9), and hip and leg raises, including scissors (five positions of two minutes each).

3. Spinal flexors: From a prone position, knee to chest slow knee hugs and hold to the count of five; and prone spinal-hip rolls (for five minutes).

4. Relaxation: Prone breathing meditative exercises to music while directing the healing energy to the midsection of the body (for ten minutes).

Figure 9 • Knee Hugs

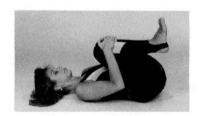

Step IX: Divine Relationships

MINERVA'S MALE COMPATIBILITY CHART

	EXCELLENT	VERY GOOD	GOOD	FAIR	POOR
ROMANCE	HERMES	ATLAS MERCURY	BACCHUS EROS	APOLLO NEPTUNE	
FRIENDSHIP	MERCURY	ATLAS EROS HERMES	BACCHUS	APOLLO NEPTUNE	
WORK	MERCURY	HERMES	ATLAS EROS	APOLLO BACCHUS NEPTUNE	

You, as a Minerva, enjoy your counterparts, gods of commerce and conventionality—Mercury, Hermes, and Atlas. They understand your sexuality, make you feel secure, and love a nurturing woman.

For the independent gods, you don't care for their venturesome spirit and emotional distance, as these characteristics threaten your peace of mind, causing you anxiety and stress. Choose your relationships wisely—be independent yourself , and all the world becomes your oyster.

Minerva, you choose female friends as you might select a support group. You flow well with most goddesses in both social activities and creative interests. You admire Artemises and Athenas in the professional arena, but seldom open up to them, for you don't like exposure, particularly if it will make you feel vulnerable. You carefully cultivate your long-term friends for what you share in common and, since these are numbered as best friends, you are loyal and trustworthy. The goddesses on this list are usually the pancreas types, other Minervas, Aphrodites, and Dianas. Interestingly, they mirror you!

Step X: The Inner Power – Meditation

Meditation Exercise

To meditate you should follow these seven basic steps:

1. Find a quiet area or corner of a room where you will not be disturbed. Near you, place a favorite religious or spiritual object, such as a statue, a crystal, or a mandala.

2. Sit on a straight-backed chair with your feet firmly planted on the floor, or sit cross-legged on the floor with your spine erect.

3. Relax your neck by rotating it, first to the right and then to the left. Tense your shoulders up; then let them fall and relax.

4. Take several deep cleansing breaths and, as you fully exhale the last one, you feel your tension leave.

5. Concentrate on a mantra (a prayer, chant, or hymn) or a monosyllabic word, such as OM.

6. Remain still for ten to fifteen minutes while attempting to control your thoughts, letting your spiritual nature nourish you.

7. Open your eyes, and come slowly back to conscious awareness. Take another deep breath, and feel yourself enveloped in the healing flow. Now you are ready to return to your outer world, feeling renewed and regenerated from the power within.

Deep Relaxation

For deep relaxation, follow these five steps:

1. No particular space is needed for this practice, just yourself.

2. Lift your head up, stick out your chin and tense your neck; then drop your head toward your chest thinking, "I relax my head and I release my mind from all tension."

3. Continue down your body in the same manner—neck, shoulders (tense, then relax); chest, arms, hands (tense, then relax); abdomen, hips, thighs (tense, then relax); and finally, legs, calves, ankles, and feet—releasing all parts of the body from tension.

4. Breathe quietly and rhythmically, feeling the healing energy flow throughout your body.

5. Now, mentally send healing to any part of your body that still feels tense, knowing that health and happiness are yours to claim.

APHRODITE

The Liberated Woman

Step I: Understanding Your Personality

The mythical Aphrodite, protectress of the Greek islands, sprang from the foam of the sea near Cyprus. She was so beautiful that she stole the hearts of all men. It was through her intercession that flowers covered the earth and storms abated. Yet, she could sometimes be manipulative when attempting to gain power over her subjects.

The Creative Wellness Aphrodite is a New Age woman who searches for independence and personal security, but through excessive striving to overcome her fears, she undermines her health.

If you have been typed an Aphrodite, you are a liberated woman with many talents. You love life's thrills. You are kind, considerate, intelligent, and artistic, always promoting fairness and equal rights. However, you often struggle needlessly with yourself through one quest or another, never totally satisfied. Your restlessness and supersensitivity can be a godsend or a curse. You can use these characteristics for creative expression, or you can let them cause you frustration that can impair your health.

As an Aphrodite, you are usually a very attractive woman. You look and dress younger than your age and project your sexuality in a stylish and unique way. The manner in which you present yourself gives a charisma that attracts men. Men love your charms and you love men in return, but you can be quite fickle with your feelings.

On the other hand, you do not handle rejection well, and criticism can defeat you. When you feel defeated, you tend to forget that you are a competent and capable woman. Even when depressed, nothing can keep you down for long. You instinctively know how to rise up and above your setbacks.

Well-known Aphrodite archetypes are Jane Fonda, Linda Evans, Princess Diana, and Vanna White. These talented women represent glamour, femininity, independence, and originality.

An Aphrodite can suffer from residual insecurities from early childhood. The absence of coddling and praise from a dysfunctional family life could leave this goddess emotionally immature and without a good image of herself. This development is the result of circumstance rather than intent, such as an absent parent or an alcoholic one. You, as an Aphrodite, may have had to confront at numerous times your disappointment with your parents' frailties or with the behavior of the men in your life, and this realization may cause some of you to deal with anger or co-dependency. You may still be trying to work out your feelings about being unjustly treated by a parental or male dominant figure.

Stress, particularly in response to emotionally charged situations involving men or your freedom of expression, can make you physically ill. Your inherent vulnerability is centered in your pancreatic enzyme reflex, which causes you emotionally induced illnesses, such as digestive disturbances, eliminative irregularities, nervous disorders, and despondency. In fact, some of you may even have a history of eating disorders, including ulcers, anorexia nervosa, and bulimia.

The inherent predisposition of pancreatic weakness need not bother you, however, if you pay close attention to your bodily needs. The Creative Wellness Plan recommends for you good nutrition above all, proper exercise, regulated time, scheduled rest management, and especially, play that provides emotional outlets. When you take care of yourself in this manner, you will have the strength to compensate for your feelings of insecurity, and you will mature gracefully in spite of yourself.

As an Aphrodite, you love being a part-time gypsy, and to meet this need, you may often take weekends off to travel. Since your interests vary and your talents are many, you should find places to go where you can be both student and social butterfly. The healing arts, as well as metaphysics, will satisfy your inner search for truth. Remember your namesake, the ancient goddess of love, for no one is more capable than you to love and be loved.

STRENGTHS AND WEAKNESSES

You are now typed as Aphrodite, the mythological goddess who embodies these strengths:

- ✧ Artistic talent
- ✧ Natural romantic inclinations
- ✧ Instinctive self-preservation skills
- ✧ Sensitivity to the needs of others
- ✧ An ability to learn quickly and remember well
- ✧ Keen sense of style, fashion, and design
- ✧ An ability to take risks

Aphrodite's inherent weaknesses are:

- ✧ Feelings of inadequacy or insecurity
- ✧ A tendency to feel depressed and defeated
- ✧ Emotional dependency (usually with the mother)
- ✧ Inability to handle criticism well
- ✧ Physical and emotional reactions to stress
- ✧ Fear of rejection
- ✧ Proclivity to overdramatize and overindulge

Step II: Reprogramming Your Psyche

APHRODITE'S AFFIRMATION

I acknowledge that in my past
I have allowed my restless spirit
To keep me from becoming a whole person
Body, mind, and soul as one.
I now accept a new understanding of myself
As a competent, secured woman,
With the faith to create a more loving,
Disciplined lifestyle
That will make me happier, healthier,
And more in tune
With the true designs for my existence.

INCENSE

Jasmine, sandalwood, lavender, gardenia, and musk

CANDLES

Orange: for self-confidence
Dark blue: for self-management
White: for spiritual awareness

Step III: Creating Healthy Nutrition

Refer to Chapter VIII, Pages 287 – 307.

Step IV: Color Support in the Wardrobe

APHRODITE'S PALETTE COLORS

Supporting Colors

Balancers	Securers	Inspirers	Protectors
Grape	Hot pink	Light pink	Magenta
Burgundy	Shrimp	Rose beige	Scarlet red
Sienna brown	Wheat	Ivory	Honey
Gold	Tan	Celery	Khaki
Cream	Lemon yellow	Mint	Emerald
Leaf green	Sea green	Eggshell blue	French gray
Pine	Turquoise	Orchid	Charcoal gray

Avoidance Colors

Aphrodite needs to avoid shades of medium to dark blue, as these colors tend to upset her pancreatic enzyme reflex balance. She likes the deeper shades of blue so as to appear in control of her life, instead of learning self-management techniques that keep her life and health in order.

Step V: Gem and Stone Strengthening

WELLNESS SUPPORT STONES
FOR APHRODITE

For the Physical Body

- Carnelian – stabilizes pancreatic function
- Dendrite and speckled agate – provide physical protection
- Jasper (all colors) – increases energy levels
- Corals and shells – foster hormonal balance

For the Emotional System

- Mother-of-pearl – alleviates mood swings
- Black onyx – prevents overreaction to stress
- Petrified woods – promote emotional stability
- Amber – protects sensitive nature

For Spiritual and Mental Awareness

- Tiger's eye – stimulates clear thinking
- Turquoise – fosters tranquillity and receptivity
- Pink quartz – increases confidence
- Crystal – enhances counseling abilities

Step VI: Scents, Herbal Elixirs, and Oils

APHRODITE'S SCENTS, ELIXIRS, AND OILS

Aphrodite's scents help to protect her from outside stresses, her elixirs maintain her youthfulness and beauty, and her oils calm her nervous system and relax her mind.

Scents	Elixirs	Oils
Jasmine	Aloe	Rose Oil
Sandalwood	Cucumber	Patchouli
Lavender	Rosemary	Olive
Gardenia	Milk and Honey	Almond
Musk	Lanolin	Musk

Step VII: Hobbies and Interests

APHRODITE'S PERSONALITY KEY

Aphrodite likes hobbies and activities that require companionship and allow chances for self-improvement. She should consider activities that both offer variety and require artistic flair.

Outdoor

- ✦ Water and snow skiing
- ✦ Entertaining outdoors
- ✦ Raising and caring for domestic animals
- ✦ Playing softball, volleyball, and badminton
- ✦ Surfing and sun bathing
- ✦ Sailing
- ✦ Taking short trips and weekend excursions

Indoor

- ✦ Creating artwork from leather, metal, or pottery
- ✦ Modern dancing
- ✦ Playing musical instruments
- ✦ Designing dresses
- ✦ Dining out
- ✦ Attending sensitivity training and awareness classes
- ✦ Going to health spas

Step VIII: *Exercises for Glandular Improvement*
Aphrodite's Exercise Routines

These exercises are meant to augment, not replace, your regular exercise routine. For further information, see the Recommended Reading section at the end of this book.

Aphrodite's exercises have been divided into four categories: warm-ups, stamina boosters, spinal flexors, and relaxation for improved immune functions and digestive enzyme performance. You, an Aphrodite, enjoy being supported by a buddy during an exercise regime; so become a member of a health spa with a friend.

1. Warm-ups: Spine and upper arm-raise stretches, feet rocking, waist bends and jumping jacks (for five minutes).

2. Stamina boosters: Torso twists, sucking-in and pushing out tummy tucks, knee to chest hugs, and hip and leg raises (four positions of $2\frac{1}{2}$ minutes each).

3. Spinal flexors: Sitting on the floor spinal twists (see Figure 10), modified sit-ups, Yoga Bow positioning of lying with stomach down, grasping ankles, and lifting legs (for five minutes).

4. Relaxation: Prone breathing meditative exercises to music while directing the healing energy to the midsection of the body (for ten minutes).

Figure 10 • Spinal Twists

Step IX: Divine Relationships

APHRODITE'S MALE COMPATIBILITY CHART

	EXCELLENT	VERY GOOD	GOOD	FAIR	POOR
ROMANCE	BACCHUS	APOLLO EROS	MERCURY NEPTUNE HERMES	ATLAS	
FRIENDSHIP		BACCHUS EROS	APOLLO NEPTUNE MERCURY HERMES	ATLAS	
WORK		APOLLO BACCHUS EROS	HERMES MERCURY NEPTUNE	ATLAS	

You, an Aphrodite, are the goddess of love and beauty, so no god would be wrong for your choosing. The most compatible to your nature are the sensitive men, Bacchus, Eros, and Apollo, as they understand your idealistic nature and seek to provide all your needs.

Since Atlas, the community father, reminds you of your own father, he is the least likely for your affections—you don't appreciate a parenting personality in romance or work. You prefer men on an equal basis, as you are an independent woman.

Aphrodite, you make the best all-around female friend when it comes to sharing another's common interests, a main ingredient in friendship. Hence, you have a varied selection to choose from among the goddesses in selecting a best friend. What might cause you trouble is long-term consistency, for you can be as changeable in the female friend arena as with males in your life. Adrenal types are first choice in work relationships; their dependability and conscientiousness support your position. So imitate Minerva, and choose your life-long buddies for the security each of you offers the other. All will benefit.

Step X: The Inner Power – Meditation
Meditation Exercise

To meditate you should follow these seven basic steps:

1. Find a quiet area or corner of a room where you will not be disturbed. Near you, place a favorite religious or spiritual object, such as a statue, a crystal, or a mandala.

2. Sit on a straight-backed chair with your feet firmly planted on the floor, or sit cross-legged on the floor with your spine erect.

3. Relax your neck by rotating it, first to the right and then to the left. Tense your shoulders up; then let them fall and relax.

4. Take several deep cleansing breaths and, as you fully exhale the last one, you feel your tension leave.

5. Concentrate on a mantra (a prayer, chant, or hymn) or a monosyllabic word, such as OM.

6. Remain still for ten to fifteen minutes while attempting to control your thoughts, letting your spiritual nature nourish you.

7. Open your eyes, and come slowly back to conscious awareness. Take another deep breath, and feel yourself enveloped in the healing flow. Now you are ready to return to your outer world, feeling renewed and regenerated from the power within.

Deep Relaxation

For deep relaxation, follow these five steps:

1. No particular space is needed for this practice, just yourself.

2. Lift your head up, stick out your chin and tense your neck; then drop your head toward your chest thinking, "I relax my head and I release my mind from all tension."

3. Continue down your body in the same manner—neck, shoulders (tense, then relax); chest, arms, hands (tense, then relax); abdomen, hips, thighs (tense, then relax); and finally, legs, calves, ankles, and feet—releasing all parts of the body from tension.

4. Breathe quietly and rhythmically, feeling the healing energy flow through your body.

5. Now, mentally send healing to any part of your body that still feels tense, knowing that health and happiness are yours to claim.

DIANA

The Civic Organizer

Step I: Understanding Your Personality

The mythical Diana, goddess of wild animals and the hunt, was the loveliest of the Roman deities. She was also considered the goddess of fertility and was invoked by all women to assure happy birth. This deity was also the preserver of youth and the protector of the lower classes, but when angered, she could disrupt the environment.

The Creative Wellness Diana is a natural manager and professional woman, but her worries about personal survival can become detrimental to her home life, career, and longevity.

If you have been typed as a Diana, you are truly a woman of greatness with a strong character and a will to succeed. These characteristics have already managed to see you through some very difficult times. If you can keep from worrying unnecessarily, your spiritual self will help you find succeess in almost any undertaking. You are smart, witty, attractive, and have an immeasurable amount of common sense. You are also extremely sensitive to yourself, a trait that some mistakenly consider conceit or selfishness.

Although you act as if personal security were not important, you prefer being secure above all else. You need to have a secure job, money in a savings account, and a safe home environment. You are not inclined to take risks, particularly financial ones, since loss affects you more than any other goddess. But as long as you are secure, you are extremely generous with your time and your money and often go out of your way to help the underdog.

The modern women who represent the Diana archetype are Elizabeth Doyle, Jeanne Kirtpatrick, Whoopi Goldberg, and the late Audrey Hepburn.

ᴄᴧ

These women, as they support humanitarian causes, represent the caring and nurturing of the masses who cannot help themselves.

As a Diana, your early personality development is partially responsible for your obsession with security. Most likely you experienced physical hardship in your formative years or watched someone close to you suffer. This deprivation could have created survival phobias that can appear at any time in your adult life, in any number of forms. Your ungrounded fears may be as grandiose as world survival or as personal as terror at the prospect of flying on an airplane or riding in an elevator. Whatever the phobia, the underlying cause is usually a childhood illusion that you must always protect yourself from harm or be protected.

You, Diana, love your home, your family life, and stable friendships. You make a good manager and counselor, but you have some difficulty exposing your own vulnerabilities for it is difficult for you to totally trust another. You like projecting an image of competence and suffer when that is threatened, as you are overly sensitive to being criticized or losing the respect of others. However, you are seldom friendless or found in a divorce court or unemployment line. Your children are fortunate to have you as a mother. So long as they respect and honor you, you are sensitive to their needs. If necessary, you will go to battle for them. You, more than any of the other goddesses, are capable of making yourself physically ill. You can be unnecessarily preoccupied with your survival fears. Any threat to your security creates undue duress, which centers in your pancreas and liver and affects your digestion and your blood chemistry, or both.

Since negative attitudes can harm your health, it is important that you understand yourself. The Creative Wellness Plan suggests for you behavior modification techniques, especially affirmations and meditation, and candle burning. These tools can be particularly helpful to a Diana who needs to reprogram her psyche. Affirmations will release what has hindered her in the past and meditation will call on the spirit within to dispel doubts and fears. Candle burning will further aid to calm the nervous system, while affirming the positive.

As you free yourself from past traumas, you will realize your true greatness. Because of what you have suffered and survived, more than any other goddess, you should be able to help humanity. In so doing, you will be honored for having the strength and conviction to complete all that you set out to accomplish.

STRENGTHS AND WEAKNESSES

You are now typed as Diana, the mythological goddess who embodies these strengths:

- ✧ Superior intellectual capabilities
- ✧ Innate resourcefulness
- ✧ A strong drive for success
- ✧ A generous and considerate nature
- ✧ Diligence with details
- ✧ Counseling and healing abilities
- ✧ Steadfast in friendship

Diana's inherent weaknesses are:

- ✧ Insecurities born from survival phobias
- ✧ Low self-esteem
- ✧ A tendency to be overanxious
- ✧ Inability to handle loss
- ✧ Physical and emotional reactions to stress
- ✧ Unrealistic concerns about the future
- ✧ Overly sensitive to outside opinions

Step II: Reprogramming Your Psyche

DIANA'S AFFIRMATIONS

I acknowledge that in my past
I have worried unnecessarily about my security
And failed to comprehend
The laws of cause and effect.
To transform my life,
I now take positive, constructive action
And put my faith in my soul
To develop a sense of well-being within myself.
Through my faith and willingness to change,
I bring health to my body,
Security to my mind,
And peace to my spirit.

INCENSE

Frangipani, sandalwood, hyacinth, gardenia, and honeysuckle

CANDLES

Orange: for emotional security
Red: for positive attitude
Green: for healing traumas of the past

Step III: Creating Healthy Nutrition

Refer to Chapter VIII, Pages 287 – 307.

Step IV: Color Support in the Wardrobe

DIANA'S PALETTE COLORS

Supporting Colors

Balancers	Securers	Inspirers	Protectors
Burgundy	Orchid	Pink	Chinese red
Brick red	Hot pink	Rose beige	Saddle brown
Honey	Sunshine yellow	Citrus yellow	Ginger
Wheat	Sand	White	Cream
Moonstone gray	Turquoise	Mint	Bright blue
Evergreen	Royal blue	Eggshell blue	Plum
Navy blue	Silver	Lilac	Charcoal gray

Avoidance Colors

Diana needs to avoid all yellow greens, such as shades of avocado, chartreuse, and jungle greens. These colors weaken her resistance to outside stress leaving her vulnerable to physical distress, excessive worry, and anxiousness.

Step V: Gem and Stone Strengthening

WELLNESS SUPPORT STONES FOR DIANA

For the Physical Body

- Sards and carnelian – aid pancreatic performance
- Moss agate (all colors) – purifies the blood
- Jasper (all colors) – increases energy levels
- Tiger's eye – enhances physical endurance

For the Emotional System

- Mother-of-pearl – stimulates nurturing qualities
- Sodalite – dispels worry
- Blue lace agate – alleviates anxiety
- Rose quartz – increases self-esteem

For Spiritual and Mental Awareness

- Turquoise – aids mental relaxation
- Jade (all colors) – increases wisdom
- Crystal – enhances healing abilities
- Pearls – foster humanitarian love

Step VI: Scents, Herbal Elixirs, and Oils

DIANA'S SCENTS, ELIXIRS, AND OILS

Diana's scents help her to relax and restore her energy, her elixirs condition her skin, and her oils support cellular rejuvenation, which aids her to remain youthful.

Scents	Elixirs	Oils
Frangipani	Herbal Mixtures	Lavender
Sandalwood	Vitamins A & D	Rose
Hyacinth	Rosemary	Peach
Gardenia	Chamomile	Peanut
Honeysuckle	Oatmeal	Patchouli

Step VII: Hobbies and Interests

DIANA'S PERSONALITY KEY

Diana enjoys noncompetitive sports in which she can excel, and she enjoys improving herself. She should consider activities that help build a sense of security and that foster self-improvement.

Outdoor

- ✧ Yachting
- ✧ Rockhounding
- ✧ Playing tennis
- ✧ Going on weekend excursions
- ✧ Swimming
- ✧ Bicycling
- ✧ Figure skating

Indoor

- ✧ Doing Yoga or T'ai Chi
- ✧ Sewing
- ✧ Bowling
- ✧ Collecting gems and rocks and making jewelry
- ✧ Tap or jazz dancing
- ✧ Watching and/or participating in adult education programs
- ✧ Playing video games

᜔

Step VIII: Excercises for Glandular Improvement
Diana's Exercise Routines

These exercises are meant to augment, not replace, your regular exercise routine. For further information , see the Recommended Reading section at the end of this book.

Diana's exercises have been divided into four categories: warm-ups, toning exercises, spinal flexors, and relaxation for improved liver function and elimination. You, a Diana, enjoy being supported during an exercise; so find yourself a personal instructor or trainer.

1. Warm-ups: At home, body stretches upon arising, abdomen massages, jog in place or on a trampoline (for five minutes).

2. Toning Exercises: Tummy tucks, modified sit-ups (see Figure 11), hip and leg raises, and chest openers with small weights (four positions of $2\frac{1}{2}$ minutes each).

3. Spinal Flexors: Sit on floor for spinal twists, head to knee bends, and stand for liver pumps of knee to chest hugs (for five minutes).

4. Relaxation: Prone breathing meditative exercises to music while directing the healing energy to the midsection of the body (for ten minutes).

Figure 11 • Modified Sit-Ups

Step IX: Divine Relationships

DIANA'S MALE COMPATIBILITY CHART

	EXCELLENT	VERY GOOD	GOOD	FAIR	POOR
ROMANCE	EROS	ATLAS BACCHUS	HERMES MERCURY	APOLLO NEPTUNE	
FRIENDSHIP		ATLAS BACCHUS EROS MERCURY	HERMES	APOLLO NEPTUNE	
WORK	MERCURY	ATLAS BACCHUS EROS MERCURY	HERMES APOLLO		NEPTUNE

You, a Diana, enjoy the gods who offer dependability and structure in your work, but Eros and Bacchus for romance and play. For long-term compatibility, only you can decide which lucky god gets your affections, since you have a bigger choice than most other goddesses.

Independent Neptune is the least likely candidate, as he can sometimes be emotionally distant and reclusive. You, too, have these tendencies and don't like to see them mirrored in another. As a transformed Diana, you can have security, a stable home life, and a loving family.

Diana, you usually select your girlfriends wisely in both your work and play, as you feel that your requirements must be a consideration in the relationship. Unfortunately, most other goddesses don't know about meeting your standards of excellence and fall short of your expectations. Some may even find themselves closed out by you over a simple matter. But, this needn't happen if you choose a sensitive Iris or Venus, an evolved Aphrodite, or another Diana like yourself to befriend you, for these women will take time to know you, share your same interests, and be a trustworthy friend long into the future.

Step X: The Inner Power – Meditation
Meditation Exercise

To meditate you should follow these seven basic steps:

1. Find a quiet area or corner of a room where you will not be disturbed. Near you, place a favorite religious or spiritual object, such as a statue, a crystal, or a mandala.

2. Sit on a straight-backed chair with your feet firmly planted on the floor, or sit cross-legged on the floor with your spine erect.

3. Relax your neck by rotating it, first to the right and then to the left. Tense your shoulders up; then let them fall and relax.

4. Take several deep cleansing breaths and, as you fully exhale the last one, you feel your tension leave.

5. Concentrate on a mantra (a prayer, chant, or hymn) or a monosyllabic word, such as OM.

6. Remain still for ten to fifteen minutes while attempting to control your thoughts, letting your spiritual nature nourish you.

7. Open your eyes, and come slowly back to conscious awareness. Take another deep breath, and feel yourself enveloped in the healing flow. Now you are ready to return to your outer world, feeling renewed and regenerated from the power within.

Deep Relaxation

For deep relaxation, follow these five steps:

1. No particular space is needed for this practice, just yourself.

2. Lift your head up, stick out your chin and tense your neck; then drop your head toward your chest thinking, "I relax my head and I release my mind from all tension."

3. Continue down your body in the same manner—neck, shoulders (tense, then relax); chest, arms, hands (tense, then relax); abdomen, hips, thighs (tense, then relax); and finally, legs, calves, ankles, and feet—releasing all parts of the body from tension.

4. Breathe quietly and rhythmically, feeling the healing energy flow throughout your body.

5. Now, mentally send healing to any part of your body that still feels tense, knowing that health and happiness are yours to claim.

CHAPTER V:

THE SEVEN GODS

APOLLO

The Charismatic Arbitrator

Step I: Understanding Your Personality

The mythical Apollo, the son of Zeus and Latona, was the god of truth. The most popular of all the gods, he was both a warrior who battled his enemies and a sensitive musician who played his golden lyre for the entertainment of the gods.

ᐦ

The Creative Wellness Apollo is a man of diplomacy who is both independent and physically strong. However, refusing to acknowledge his emotional needs can shorten his life span.

If you have been identified as an Apollo, you probably enjoy being called a god, since you already know you are one or believe you should be one. You were born with great physical attributes—height, proportion, agility—and the charisma of a natural leader. You consider yourself talented and capable and admire skill in others as well.

You have many characteristics that help you succeed at almost any undertaking: You are ambitious and energetic; you are an aggressive warrior; you love to win. What you do not like about yourself are things that others don't like either. You can sometimes be insensitive to the feelings of another, realizing only too late that you've hurt them deeply. Although you may feel some remorse and try to repair the harm, most often you just walk away, rationalizing that the person you've hurt must have deserved it. To compensate your guilt, you tend to indulge and seek pleasure where you can find it.

Your insensitivity is only a protective shield. You probably developed it in early childhood to defend yourself against an overbearing personality or from undue authoritative demands placed upon you as a youth. It gave you a way to mask your sensitive nature so that the world—and your parents in particular—would not see your vulnerability. This deceptive self-presentation soon developed into a self-control that gives you an appearance of emotional detachment. Though this self-containment helps you succeed in business and in certain social situations, you well know the conflict it sometimes creates inside yourself. Often, you wish you could throw convention to the wind, pack your bags, and leave all responsibility behind you.

You are the greatest of communicators and arbitrators. Your distinctive voice can mesmerize an audience and your sense of humor entertains them as well. Apollo feels at home on stage, in the courtroom, and in the executive boardroom. He usually chooses a professional career for he has innate intelligence and is charisma personified.

Recognizable personalities who fit the Apollo archetype are Ronald Reagan, Ted Turner, Tom Selleck, and Al Gore. These men represent humor, stardom, executive ability, and sensitivity to the needs of the populace.

As an Apollo, you often exercise will over emotion and this can have a negative effect on your body, particularly after middle age. It can create an imbalance in your thyroid system that interferes with your metabolism and with your ability to rejuvenate yourself. If not corrected, the imbalance can speed up the aging process.

You can counter this vulnerability by turning your strong urge to control life's opportunities or stresses into learning how to express your feelings. You can also discover ways of developing your intuition so as to become more aware of your inner feelings and the sensitivities of others. Another constructive use of your positive qualities is to let your natural tact help you resolve social conflicts diplomatically, using your charms for good and positive results, not destructive purposes.

Changing your behavior is imperative if you want to maintain good health, especially if you are already showing symptoms of thyroid irregularity, such as metabolism disorders, circulation problems, and digestive disturbances. Chronic sinus headaches, tension in your neck, or waning sexual potency can be the early signs that you need to change your habits. Finding a more creative way to express your feelings counteracts your overly controlled nature. Give your emotions a healing outlet—for example, take up an Eastern physical discipline, such as Yoga or T'ai Chi, join a choir, or a dance class, get involved in charity work, or do them all.

It is your nature as an Apollo to love the limelight, so use your influence to set a good example. People desire your company. Be sensitive to others and to yourself. Abandon your shield and use your good will to make a difference in the world—remember, it's good karma!

STRENGTHS AND WEAKNESSES

You are now typed as Apollo, the mythical god who embodies these strengths:

- ✦ Superb communication abilities
- ✦ Keen intellectual attributes
- ✦ Diplomacy and tact
- ✦ A natural warrior
- ✦ An ability to make realistic value judgments
- ✦ A good sense of humor
- ✦ Good athletic skills

Apollo's weaknesses are:

- ✦ Repressed sensitivity because of demanding parental influence
- ✦ A lack of understanding of his inner feelings
- ✦ Excessive need for self-gratification
- ✦ A disregard for the sensitivity of another
- ✦ A tendency to be overly aggressive
- ✦ Suffers from stress-induced physical symptoms
- ✦ Escapist inclinations

Step II: Reprogramming Your Psyche

APOLLO'S AFFIRMATION

I acknowledge that in the past
I have disregarded my sensitive nature,
Which has caused me to develop
An imbalanced lifestyle.
I now pledge to honor my total self,
Body, mind, and soul as one.
Knowing this reality,
I will become more sensitive
To the needs of myself and others
And bring peace and harmony into my life

INCENSE

Sandalwood, pine, lavender, citrus (lemon/lime), frangipani

CANDLES

Red: for emotional freedom
Green: for healing the past
Lavender: for heightened sensitivity

Step III: Creating Healthy Nutrition

Refer to Chapter VI, Pages 229 – 246.

Step IV: Color Support in the Wardrobe

APOLLO'S PALETTE COLORS

Supporting Colors

Balancers	Securers	Inspirers	Protectors
Dark brown	Burgundy	Peach	Charcoal gray
Saddle brown	Melon	Tan	Pewter gray
Sienna	Apricot	Celery green	Rust
Khaki	Lemon yellow	Mint	Pumpkin
Forest green	Cream	Eggshell blue	Gold
Navy blue	Leaf green	Mauve	Sunshine yellow
Slate blue	Turquoise	Silver	Wheat

Avoidance Colors

Apollo needs to avoid all bright reds, including cardinal and fire-engine red. These colors give a false sense of power, which leads him to repress his sensitivity and become overly defensive. They should never be worn around the neck, as in a tie, for these reds increase tension and stress, as well as depleting his energy.

Step V: Gem and Stone Strengthening

WELLNESS SUPPORT STONES FOR APOLLO

For the Physical Body

- Indian agate – maintains physical strength
- Petrified wood or picture agate – supports sexual stamina

- Jasper (all colors except red) – increases energy levels
- Garnet – regulates metabolism

For the Emotional System

- Mother-of-pearl – fosters emotional sensitivity
- Mexican lace agate – prevents depression
- Moonstone – encourages self-love
- Amber – protects against stress

For Spiritual and Mental Awareness

- Blue lace agate – fosters mental relaxation
- Lapis lazuli – expands mental faculties
- Malachite – unites reasoning and intuition
- Tiger's eye – provides clear discernment

Step VI: Scents, Herbal Elixirs, and Oils

APOLLO'S SCENTS, ELIXIRS, AND OILS

Apollo's scents aid him to release his tension, his elixirs prevent premature aging, and his oils improve circulation and support skin rejuvenation.

Scents	Elixirs	Oils
Lavender	Aloe	Wheat germ
Pine	Cucumber	Vitamin E
Frangipani	Avocado	Almond
Lemon/Lime	Myrrh	Jojoba
Sandalwood	Lanolin	Sage

Step VII: Hobbies and Interests

APOLLO'S PERSONALITY KEY

Apollo loves competition and activities that require athletic skills, especially when they are set outdoors and when he has the star role. He should consider activities that give him the chance to shine.

Outdoor

- ✧ Fishing competitions—deep-sea and stream
- ✧ Water and snow skiing
- ✧ Playing polo or horse racing
- ✧ Mountain climbing and rappelling
- ✧ Playing football, basketball, and baseball
- ✧ Jogging and long distance running
- ✧ Traveling on short trips

Indoor

- ✧ Using home entertainment such as video machines and stereo
- ✧ Being a fine arts and theater patron
- ✧ Practicing martial arts
- ✧ Leading civic organizations
- ✧ Watching indoor sports
- ✧ Playing racquetball and squash
- ✧ Playing poker and Trivial Pursuit

Step VIII: *Exercises for Glandular Improvement*

Apollo's Exercise Routines

These exercises are meant to augment, not replace, your regular exercise routine. For further information , see the Recommended Reading section at the end of this book.

Apollo's exercises have been divided into four categories: glandular strengthening, overall toning, relaxation, and rejuvenation to prevent premature aging, poor metabolism, and circulation.

1. Glandular Strengthening: Early morning spinal stretches, head, neck, and shoulder rolls (for five minutes).

2. Overall Toning: Jog in place or out-of-doors morning run, followed by upper torso weight lifting and push-ups for strengthening muscle tone (for ten minutes).

3. Relaxation: Yoga shoulder stand pose, followed by the Yoga plough pose (see Figure 12) (for two to five minutes).

4. Rejuvenation: Deep relaxation (see Step X) and creative visualization to release tension and stimulate healing flow throughout the body. Relaxation techniques to be practiced in a prone position (for ten minutes).

Figure 12 • Yoga Plough Pose

Step IX: Divine Relationships

APOLLO'S FEMALE COMPATIBILITY CHART

	EXCELLENT	VERY GOOD	GOOD	FAIR	POOR
ROMANCE		VENUS APHRODITE	MINERVA	ARTEMIS ATHENA DIANA	
FRIENDSHIP		VENUS APHRODITE	ARTEMIS ATHENA DIANA IRIS	MINERVA	
WORK		ARTEMIS ATHENA VENUS	ARTEMIS VENUS IRIS	MINERVA	

You, as Apollo, find all women attractive, but you get along best with Venus and Aphrodite in the romance department, and Artemis and Athena on work-related projects.

The pancreas type goddesses are only average in your estimation as friends and working peers, since you prefer sensitive and more independent women to inspire you. Apollo, the diplomat and the charismatic arbitrator, likes his mate to be a goddess, only her role is second in command to his, otherwise, he might turn his warring spirit toward her.

Apollo, you choose your male friends as a coach would select football players to fill positions on this team. You usually don't look for emotional support in male companionship, reserving this right for the opposite sex. Bacchus, Eros, and Atlas—the physically oriented Gods—you consider peers professionally and at play. You seldom select Apollos or Mercurys as allies, for these men, you feel, vie for your position, and you are too protective naturally to let them in. You admire the philosophy of Neptune and the diligence of Hermes but when all is said and done, Apollo's motto is "I did it my way."

Step X: The Inner Power – Meditation
Meditation Exercise

To meditate you should follow these seven basic steps:

1. Find a quiet area or corner of a room where you will not be disturbed. Near you, place a favorite religious or spiritual object, such as a statue, a crystal, or a mandala.

2. Sit on a straight-backed chair with your feet firmly planted on the floor, or sit cross-legged on the floor with your spine erect.

3. Relax your neck by rotating it, first to the right and then to the left. Tense your shoulders up; then let them fall and relax.

4. Take several deep cleansing breaths and, as you fully exhale the last one, you feel your tension leave.

5. Concentrate on a mantra (a prayer, chant, or hymn) or a monosyllabic word, such as OM.

6. Remain still for ten to fifteen minutes while attempting to control your thoughts, letting your spiritual nature nourish you.

7. Open your eyes, and come slowly back to conscious awareness. Take another deep breath, and feel yourself enveloped in the healing flow. Now you are ready to return to your outer world, feeling renewed and regenerated from the power within.

Deep Relaxation

For deep relaxation, follow these five steps:

1. No particular space is needed for this practice, just yourself.

2. Lift your head up, stick out your chin and tense your neck; then drop your head toward your chest thinking, "I relax my head and I release my mind from all tension."

3. Continue down your body in the same manner—neck, shoulders (tense, then relax); chest, arms, hands (tense, then relax); abdomen, hips, thighs (tense, then relax); and finally, legs, calves, ankles, and feet—releasing all parts of the body from tension.

4. Breathe quietly and rhythmically, feeling the healing energy flow throughout your body.

5. Now, mentally send healing to any part of your body that still feels tense, knowing that health and happiness are yours to claim.

MERCURY

The Resourceful Executive

Step I: Understanding Your Personality

The mythical Mercury, Roman god of trade, commerce, and merchants fostered secured economics at home and abroad. This popular god was considered the most resourceful of all the gods, but was regarded as having a mother complex, being associated frequently with his mother, Maia.

The Creative Wellness Mercury is the corporate executive who loves a secure home. He has executive decision-making abilities par excellence. However, he has a tendency to repress his emotions and create a split between what he thinks and what he feels.

If you have been typed as a Mercury, you are ambitious, aggressive, intellectual, and sensitive. Although not a social conformist, you usually like your home and business run in a structured way. You love science and research as you have an inquiring mind. You can be practical, determined, and straightforward, but you can also be grasping, unsure of yourself, and dictatorial.

Emotional deprivation in early childhood begot by the absence of a parent, or by being one of many children who had to compete with another sibling for parental affection, has caused you to develop in one of two ways: Either you compensated for the lack of emotional gratification by vying for the affection of one parent over the other or you withdrew completely from both parents to a new safe space within yourself. In either case, you were left with a need to control, a need that at times can drive you to erratic behavior. Therefore, you are comfortable in a position of authority, but have a tendency at times to be insensitive to the feelings of another.

As a result of your childhood, you may have focused your energies on developing your intellect. You have a naturally inquisitive mind and are wonderful at inventing, analyzing, solving problems, and teaching others. Your logic is your greatest asset and can support you in any profession that you choose.

Renowned gentlemen who image the archetypal Mercury are Lee Iacocca, General Colin Powell, Kirk Douglas, and Jonas Salk, M.D. These men exhibit extraordinary qualities of overcoming early life situations and have become outstanding leaders in their fields of endeavor.

Physically, Mercury, you are a survivor. Normally you don't fall prey to minor illnesses and stresses, unless your emotional life is in an uproar. When it is, you are susceptible to major thyroid imbalances. These metabolic imbalances can lead to obesity, hypertension, and multiple digestive dysfunctions. Luckily, you have an inherent above-average constitution and can maintain your health, once you learn to respect your emotional sensitivities and cope with your stresses.

As a Mercury, you love home life and prefer your mate to be the homemaker, raising your children. When disillusioned in love, you will remove yourself and, rather than repeat your mistake, choose to remain unattached and distant from women thereafter. If you can deal with your past traumas, however, you can free yourself of this isolation. Lucky is the woman who earns your respect and admiration. As long as the two of you are a couple, she will never cease to be admired and respected.

As a boss or colleague, your success drive isn't always appreciated by others. You, Mercury, find it difficult to work in a subordinate position or to be criticized by those you feel inferior to yourself. So, The Creative Wellness Plan recommends you honor your sensitivity, forgive others for their weaknesses, and acknowledge your own contributions. You need to focus your attention on your own inner security, paying less attention to how others view you. You can do this by reprogramming yourself with behavior modification tools: affirmation, candle burning, meditation, and spiritual-involvement activities.

The uniqueness of Mercury assures that you will never stop learning or living your life to the fullest. You can go on to a ripe old age if you take care of your body. You are spiritually inclined to tackle global problems and are usually prepared to handle them. If every world leader were as competent as you, there would be unbroken peaceful advancement in the arts, sciences, and educational fields, with untold benefits to humankind.

STRENGTHS AND WEAKNESSES

You are now typed as Mercury, the mythical god who embodies these strengths:

- ❖ A motivation for achievement
- ❖ A keen intellect
- ❖ The capacity to accomplish self-established goals
- ❖ An inherent strong physical constitution
- ❖ Executive decision-making abilities
- ❖ Love of home and family
- ❖ An appreciation of the finer things of life

Mercury's weaknesses are:

- ❖ A tendency to repress emotions
- ❖ Inclination to be manipulative
- ❖ An obsessive drive to overwork
- ❖ Prideful attitudes hiding insecurities
- ❖ Chronic worrying that undermines health
- ❖ Defensive to criticism
- ❖ Puts his own needs before another's

Step II: Reprogramming Your Psyche

MERCURY'S AFFIRMATION

I acknowledge that in the past
I have allowed my insecurities
To foster an overcontrolling nature,
Which denies my sensitivities.
In acknowledging this weakness,
I affirm to change myself,
So that in the future
I will make the right choices
To live a more balanced life.
This affirmation restores my faith in others,
And brings peace to my soul.

INCENSE

Honeysuckle, sandalwood, spice, pine, and patchouli

CANDLES

Berry red: for emotional security
Light blue: for calming the psyche
White: for uplifting the spirit

Step III: Creating Healthy Nutrition

Refer to Chapter VI, Pages 229 – 246.

Step IV: Color Support in the Wardrobe

MERCURY'S PALETTE COLORS

Supporting Colors

Balancers	Securers	Inspirers	Protectors
Dark brown	Chinese red	Rose beige	Charcoal gray
Saddle brown	Shrimp	Peach	Pewter
Sienna	Apricot	Lemon	Tan
Khaki	Ivory	Celery	Rust
Pine green	Nile green	Mint	Wheat
Navy blue	Teal	Sky blue	Gold
Slate blue	Turquoise	Mauve	Sunshine yellow

Avoidance Colors

Mercury needs to avoid all deep reds, such as burgundy and wine, because these tend to overstimulate his need to control and can distract him from being sensitive to the needs of another. Simultaneously, these reds can aggravate an already hypertensive personality.

Step V: Gem and Stone Strengthening

WELLNESS SUPPORT STONES FOR MERCURY

For the Physical Body

- Carnelian – maintains pancreatic function
- Bloodstone – improves circulation
- Indian agate – supports energy levels
- Garnet – regulates metabolism

For the Emotional System

- Mexican lace agate – increases emotional satisfaction
- Moonstone – encourages self-love
- Black onyx – protects emotional sensitivity
- Jasper (all colors except red) – stabilizes emotions

For Spiritual and Mental Awareness

- Blue lace agate – fosters mental relaxation
- Malachite – unites reasoning and intuition
- Lapis lazuli – expands mental faculties
- Crystal – heightens inner awareness

Step VI: Scents, Herbal Elixirs, and Oils

MERCURY'S SCENTS, ELIXIRS, AND OILS

Mercury's scents aid him to balance mind and emotions, his elixirs help him feel more youthful, and his oils help him restore his energy.

Scents	Elixirs	Oils
Honeysuckle	Chamomile	Jojoba
Spice	Aloe	Lemon/Lime
Sandalwood	Mint	Vitamine E
Patchouli	Cocoa butter	Lavender
Pine	Vitamins A & D	Almond

Step VII: Hobbies and Interests

MERCURY'S PERSONALITY KEY

Mercury appreciates hobbies and activities that require problem solving and competition. He should consider activities that require the use of his intellectual skills.

Outdoor

- ✧ Yachting and sailing
- ✧ Golfing
- ✧ Deep-sea fishing
- ✧ Traveling abroad (first class)
- ✧ Jogging
- ✧ Playing tennis
- ✧ Working on or collecting automobiles

Indoor

- ✧ Attending fitness or health club
- ✧ Attending classical music performances
- ✧ Art collecting and judging
- ✧ Completing crossword puzzles and reading mystery novels
- ✧ Participating in encounter or philosophic study groups
- ✧ Playing bridge
- ✧ Programming computers and playing video games

Step VIII: *Exercises for Glandular Improvement*

Mercury's Exercise Routines

These exercises are meant to augment, not replace, your regular exercise routine. For further information , see the Recommended Reading section at the end of this book.

Mercury's exercises have been divided into four categories: warm-ups, toning exercises, rejuvenation, and relaxation to prevent high blood pressure and improve thyroid functioning.

1. Warm-ups: Early morning spinal stretches; head, neck, and shoulder rolls (see Figure 13); hip twists and jumping jacks (for five minutes).

2. Toning exercises: Jog in place or out-of-doors morning run, followed by upper torso weight lifting, push-ups and sit-ups for strengthening muscle tone (for ten minutes).

3. Rejuvenation: Bike-riding or Nautilus walking equipment exercise, or step-aerobics (for time desired).

4. Relaxation: Tape or music meditation with practices of releasing body tension with breath control (for ten minutes).

Figure 13 • *Head, Neck, and Shoulder Rolls*

Step IX: Divine Relationships

MERCURY'S FEMALE COMPATIBILITY CHART

	EXCELLENT	VERY GOOD	GOOD	FAIR	POOR
ROMANCE	MINERVA	APHRODITE DIANA	VENUS	ARTEMIS ATHENA	IRIS
FRIENDSHIP	DIANA	MINERVA	APHRODITE ARTEMIS VENUS	ATHENA IRIS	
WORK	MINERVA	APHRODITE DIANA	ARTEMIS VENUS IRIS	ATHENA	

You, as a Mercury, make the best husband for a number of the goddesses, as you admire and respect women in general. For a business associate, a pancreas type female suits your executive nature without stressing you, as she is sensitive to your needs and practical in her work.

Ambitious and aggressive females you don't care for at all, as these women can mirror your innate weaknesses making you feel insecure. Lucky is the woman who earns your admiration and honor, for you will be treated as an Adam and she, your Eve.

Mercury, you choose your friends in both work and play as a corporate infra-structure. Success-oriented gods such as Hermes, Eros, Bacchus, and other Mercurys, you count on as friends and compatriots, seldom allowing pettiness to interfere with loyalty. True friendship means to you respect, honor, and dependability. Amazingly, you have lifelong male friends even if your marital or professional status changes. Those lucky gods that can be considered a Mercury's chosen few, have a soul-to-soul, as well as mind-to-mind connection, and you work at keeping it that way.

Step X: The Inner Power – Meditation

Meditation Exercise

To meditate you should follow these seven basic steps:

1. Find a quiet area or corner of a room where you will not be disturbed. Near you, place a favorite religious or spiritual object, such as a statue, a crystal, or a mandala.

2. Sit on a straight-backed chair with your feet firmly planted on the floor, or sit cross-legged on the floor with your spine erect.

3. Relax your neck by rotating it, first to the right and then to the left. Tense your shoulders up; then let them fall and relax.

4. Take several deep cleansing breaths and, as you fully exhale the last one, you feel your tension leave.

5. Concentrate on a mantra (a prayer, chant, or hymn) or a monosyllabic word, such as OM.

6. Remain still for ten to fifteen minutes, while attempting to control your thoughts, letting your spiritual nature nourish you.

7. Open your eyes, and come slowly back to conscious awareness. Take another deep breath, and feel yourself enveloped in the healing flow. Now you are ready to return to your outer world, feeling renewed and regenerated from the power within.

Deep Relaxation

For deep relaxation, follow these five steps:

1. No particular space is needed for this practice, just yourself.

2. Lift your head up, stick out your chin, and tense your neck; then drop your head toward your chest thinking, "I relax my head and I release my mind from all tension."

3. Continue down your body in the same manner—neck, shoulders (tense, then relax); chest, arms, hands (tense, then relax); abdomen, hips, thighs (tense, then relax); and finally, legs, calves, ankles, and feet—releasing all parts of the body from tension.

4. Breathe quietly and rhythmically, feeling the healing energy flow throughout your body.

5. Now, mentally send healing to any part of your body that still feels tense, knowing that health and happiness are yours to claim.

NEPTUNE

The Futurist

Step I: Understanding Your Personality

The mythical Neptune, the Roman god who governed the Earth's waters, was the master of all marine life. He gave horses to man and guarded the environment, both atmospheric and earthly. His character was as gentle as the dolphin and as violent as an earthquake.

The Creative Wellness Neptune is a natural philosopher and problem solver. He looks to the future with a deep appreciation of the past. He enjoys the outdoors, and like his namesake, he loves water to live by or participate in as a sport, such as fishing, swimming, and boating. When he denies himself his rest and play, he can easily lose his sense of reality to his physical and emotional needs.

If you have been typed as a Neptune, you are probably more mature than most men your age. You appear calm, cool, and in total control. This maturity enhances your positive traits: forthrightness, sensitivity, compassion, and understanding.

However, you were not always at this age of wisdom. As a youth, you were either an outgoing playboy, or an adventurous risk-taker. As you grew older, you matured and with this maturity developed other traits: farsightedness, discernment, and a great respect for human existence. The latter, raising your level of consciousness, gives you both philosophic and philanthropic tendencies. Truly, the fate of the world should rest in your hands.

Identifiable men who image the archetypal Neptune in today's world are George Bush, Norman Schwarzkopf, Charlton Heston, and John Naisbitt, (author of *Megatrends*). These experienced personalities demonstrate farsightedness and willingness to follow their beliefs.

You, as a Neptune, when young, may have had difficulty dealing with your sensitivity. It must have been frustrating being a sensitive youth in a society when men were not supposed to show emotions. You were also susceptible to being dominated by a possessive female, probably your mother, who may have been widowed or divorced. She placed unusual demands on you and wanted your unqualified love in return.

You learned to deal with outside dominance by stifling your emotions, a process that set you up for future health problems. This repression, combined with your strong sense of conscience caused your adrenal glands to work overtime, exhausting them. And this, in turn, affected the pituitary/adrenal/sex-gland hormone function, particularly when under emotional duress. You probably have always had to deal with allergy and sinus problems and today may even suffer from hypertension and circulatory problems.

As a Neptune, you make a superb problem solver, counselor, and statistician. You love to imagine creative ways to help others solve their issues. Most of you take great pride in knowing that you have your feet firmly planted on the ground but can let your imaginations soar, since you have the ability to see past, present, and future simultaneously. Therefore, your love of history, flying, collecting treasures from the past, and planning for the future, enhance your all "sighted" personality.

Because of your need for independence, you may experience difficulty with female relationships. The demands from your mother affected you emotionally, and to compensate, you easily become discouraged with needy women or set yourself up for disappointment in romantic alliances.

The Creative Wellness Plan recommends for a Neptune first, the awareness of the psychological undercurrents that make him susceptible to hypertension and other illnesses; and secondly, the understanding of how he must live to prevent poor health from ensuing. This can be done by simple counseling, by following a low-cholesterol diet, by engaging in outdoor activities, by scheduling rest and play, and most importantly, by taking time for meditation and contemplation.

A healthy Neptune is the wisest of statesman whose sensitivity qualifies him as the sage of modern times. Others may have concerns about the future, but you with your higher understanding will always be there to put their fears to bed.

STRENGTHS AND WEAKNESSES

You are now typed as Neptune, the mythical god who embodies these strengths:

- ✧ A creative imagination
- ✧ Natural intuition
- ✧ An innate sense of duty
- ✧ Professional independence
- ✧ Talent in planning and problem solving
- ✧ A love of history, philosophy, and nature
- ✧ A humanitarian father figure

Neptune's weaknesses are:

- ✧ Self-defeatist attitudes in relationships with women
- ✧ Repressed anger from inner conflicts
- ✧ Escapist and reckless tendencies
- ✧ A vulnerability to poor health habits
- ✧ An inability to release past traumas
- ✧ A tendency to feel frustrated
- ✧ An unawareness of personal endurance levels

Step II: Reprogramming Your Psyche

NEPTUNE'S AFFIRMATION

I acknowledge that in the past
I have not been wise in handling
My health requirements,
And allowed my frustrations
And self-defeatist attitudes
To affect my health.
By changing my daily habits
And transforming my attitude,
I create for myself a healthy body,
A balanced mind, and a peaceful spirit
That will assure me longevity and a fulfilled life.

INCENSE

Lavender, bayberry, pine, sandalwood, musk

CANDLES

Red: for positive attitude
Dark blue: for self-management
Green: for healing the past

Step III: Creating Healthy Nutrition

Refer to Chapter VII, Pages 266 – 285.

Step IV: Color Support in the Wardrobe

NEPTUNE'S PALETTE COLORS

Supporting Colors

Balancers	Securers	Inspirers	Protectors
Saddle brown	Cherry red	Lilac	Charcoal gray
Brick red	Pumpkin	Rose beige	Felt gray
Ginger	Peach	Tan	Khaki
Gold	Sunshine yellow	Ivory	Honey
Olive	Cream	Lemon yellow	Salmon
Pine	Mint	Celery	Burgundy
Slate blue	Wedgwood blue	Eggshell blue	Plum

Avoidance Colors

Neptune needs to avoid all dark blues, especially royal blues, since these shades cause him to weaken physically and leave him vulnerable to external stresses. Dark blues tend to give him a false sense of being in control, but support only his mind and not his body.

Step V: Gem and Stone Strengthening

WELLNESS SUPPORT STONES FOR NEPTUNE

For the Physical Body

- Bloodstone – improves circulation
- Amber – protects the adrenal system

- Coral (all colors) – stimulates hormonal production
- Red moss agate, red jasper, or plume agate – increases sexual stamina

For the Emotional System

- Rhodochrosite – restores depleted emotions
- Moonstone – encourages self-love
- Mother-of-pearl – promotes self-nurturing
- Shells and fossils – reduce nervous tension

For Spiritual and Mental Awareness

- Tiger's eye or falcon's eye – gives clear insight and objectivity
- Amethyst – increases intuitive awareness
- Jade (all colors) – helps develop wisdom
- Tourmaline – provides peace of mind

Step VI: Scents, Herbal Elixirs, and Oils

NEPTUNE'S SCENTS, ELIXIRS, AND OILS

Neptune's scents help support his intuitive nature, his elixirs aid skin rejuvenation, and his oils foster overall relaxation.

Scents	Elixirs	Oils
Lavender	Aloe	Almond
Bayberry	Cucumber	Olive
Pine	Rose Water & Glycerine	Mineral
Musk	Comfrey	Lanolin
Sandalwood	Cocoa butter	Vitamine E

Step VII: Hobbies and Interests

NEPTUNE'S PERSONALITY KEY

Neptune has an interest in the meaning of life and needs to find activities that allow expression of his philosophical side. He should consider emotionally and spiritually stimulating activities.

Outdoor

- ✧ Treasure and artifact hunting
- ✧ White-water rafting
- ✧ Boat or plane piloting
- ✧ Traveling, especially on historical tours
- ✧ Golfing
- ✧ Gardening or caring for plants
- ✧ Swimming

Indoor

- ✧ Studying esoteric or metaphysical ideas
- ✧ Visiting art exhibits, especially folk or primitive art
- ✧ Coin, stamp, and book collecting
- ✧ Bird watching and star gazing
- ✧ Restoring antique cars and furniture
- ✧ Speculating in the money market
- ✧ Writing – songs, poetry, and journal entries

Step VIII: *Exercises for Glandular Improvement*

Neptune's Exercise Routines

These exercises are meant to augment, not replace, your regular exercise routine. For further information , see the Recommended Reading section at the end of this book.

Neptune's exercises have been divided into three categories: warm-ups, chest strengthening, and deep relaxation, followed by an out-of-door exercise for improved circulation, such as brisk walks, swimming, or hiking.

1. Warm-ups: Overall spine stretches, loosening upper torso by arm raises and push-offs, twists, and shoulder-to-floor bends (for ten minutes).

2. Chest strengthening: Lifting weights (see Figure 14), breathing exercises, and step or stair climbing (for ten minutes).

3. Deep relaxation: From a seated position—spine straight, hands in lap—meditative relaxation, directing healing energy to head, adrenal, and base of spine (for five to ten minutes).

Figure 14 • Weight Lifting

Step IX: Divine Relationships

NEPTUNE'S FEMALE COMPATIBILITY CHART

	EXCELLENT	VERY GOOD	GOOD	FAIR	POOR
ROMANCE		VENUS APHRODITE IRIS	ATHENA MINERVA	ARTEMIS	DIANA
FRIENDSHIP		APHRODITE IRIS	ARTEMIS ATHENA MINERVA VENUS	DIANA	
WORK		APHRODITE ARTEMIS IRIS	ATHENA VENUS MINERVA	DIANA ARTEMIS	

You, as a Neptune prefer the adrenal type goddesses, as you require her sensitivities, and love her vagarious lifestyle. You prefer a peaceful relationship with a woman, rather than one of conflict, because your home is your castle.

Neptune reaches for a kindred soul, or not at all, because there is little physical attraction without the spiritual. You embrace women that have the same appreciation of life as you, and don't mind sharing your intimacies and dreams with them across the table. Don't be a rescuer or transformer of needy women, leave that to other gods more qualified.

Neptune, you prefer your male friends to be a "buddy system," there for you when you call, noninvasive when you don't. At work you appreciate Mercury, Apollo, Bacchus, and Eros, as these can be your intellectual peers. However, your social friendship club is exclusive, including only those who acknowledge that there is more to life than just striving for material success. Even though you are seldom intimate with men, you like sharing your varied interests, traveling, exploring, collecting. Often, these men are the same types as yourself, or the younger Bacchus or Eros, gods to whom you can play the teacher.

Step X: The Inner Power – Meditation

Meditation Exercise

To meditate you should follow these seven basic steps:

1. Find a quiet area or corner of a room where you will not be disturbed. Near you, place a favorite religious or spiritual object, such as a statue, a crystal, or a mandala.

2. Sit on a straight-backed chair with your feet firmly planted on the floor, or sit cross-legged on the floor with your spine erect.

3. Relax your neck by rotating it, first to the right and then to the left. Tense your shoulders up; then let them fall and relax.

4. Take several deep cleansing breaths and, as you fully exhale the last one, you feel your tension leave.

5. Concentrate on a mantra (a prayer, chant, or hymn) or a monosyllabic word, such as OM.

6. Remain still for ten to fifteen minutes while attempting to control your thoughts, letting your spiritual nature nourish you.

7. Open your eyes, and come slowly back to conscious awareness. Take another deep breath, and feel yourself enveloped in the healing flow. Now you are ready to return to your outer world, feeling renewed and regenerated from the power within.

Deep Relaxation

For deep relaxation, follow these five steps:

1. No particular space is needed for this practice, just yourself.

2. Lift your head up, stick out your chin, and tense your neck; then drop your head toward your chest thinking, "I relax my head and I release my mind from all tension."

3. Continue down your body in the same manner—neck, shoulders (tense, then relax); chest, arms, hands (tense, then relax); abdomen, hips, thighs (tense, then relax); and finally, legs, calves, ankles, and feet—releasing all parts of the body from tension.

4. Breathe quietly and rhythmically, feeling the healing energy flow throughout your body.

5. Now, mentally send healing to any part of your body that still feels tense, knowing that health and happiness are yours to claim.

BACCHUS

The Perceptive Communicator

Step I: Understanding Your Personality

The mythical Bacchus, a Roman god, also named Dionysus to the Greeks, was the son of Zeus and a mortal woman. He was the lord of fruitfulness and vegetation, known as the god of wine and ecstasy. He was originally a joyful and healing god, but some of his priests forming a cult, made him a god of revelry. And for this reason he came to represent both good and evil.

The Creative Wellness Bacchus is a natural communicator and salesman, but tends to undermine his health if he focuses too much on gratifying his appetites. He is usually sexy, attractive, and youthful in appearance. His smile charms men and women alike for he has innate good humor.

If you have typed a Bacchus, you are basically an admirable, responsible, and trustworthy individual. At the same time, you are fun-loving and have an almost childlike demeanor. Your innocent look makes you appear as if you don't have a care in the world.

You are popular with the opposite sex and you know it. You have finesse, diplomacy, winning magnetism, and you usually know when to be quiet for you are a good listener. However, women generally have to earn your admiration and your enduring affection. Of all the gods, you are the one who prefers a liberated woman and you will make a marvelously loyal spouse. She will never lack anything as you want to supply her with every material comfort. You may leave the philosophy of life to others, but you manage the everyday world beautifully.

Men who image the archetypal personality of Bacchus are Bill Murray, Michael J. Fox, Magic Johnson, and Og Mandino (author of *The Greatest Salesman In The World*). These men exhibit the power of persuasive communication in humor, acting, sports, and writing.

As a Bacchus, you probably started out as an idealistic trusting child, with a sensitive and loving nature. This made you vulnerable to disillusionment, when your parents fell short of your ideals. You might have had a weak, placid father or a distant or absent mother who showed too little attention to your needs. In either case, you had to learn to cope as best you could by building your self-confidence on your own. Hence, stress affected you adversely even as a child, making you vulnerable to mood swings, as well as many childhood illnesses, some of which may have been a psychosomatic way of attempting to get the attention you craved.

Later though, as a maturing Bacchus, you compensated by developing one of two lifestyle patterns or a combination of both. You might have formed a self-defeatist attitude setting yourself up for failure, or you felt a need to seek escape through food, sex, drugs, or drink—all similar forms of self-gratification. Another way you might have matured is a far more positive way, by assuming an adult role at a very young age. Though the latter might have saved you from a self-destructive lifestyle, it burdened you with overresponsibility, and consequently drove you to a determined quest for power, material success, and a fulfillment of personal dreams.

You thrive on competition, both mental and physical. You like to win in sales, promotions, on the basketball court, and on the golf course. Skill is very important to a Bacchus because this personifies self-confidence, but you should always remain cautious of developing addictive habits, such as gambling for quick money and success. In love, you are an eternal romanticist, remaining amorous right on into your golden years. When disappointed in love, however, you picture the dark side of Bacchus for you can be very insensitive and cruel to those who have hurt you.

Luckily, as a Bacchus, you probably inherited the good genes of your parents and so have few genetic defects. Your potential vulnerabilities are centered in your lifestyle. Up to age thirty-five, you are usually free of serious health problems, except those minor illnesses caused by stress, such as food allergies, environmental sensitivities, and some gastric distresses. After middle-age, you are susceptible to developing any of a number of serious problems—heart, prostate, kidney, and bladder.

But don't worry Bacchus. It's not too late to prevent these health impairments from developing. The Creative Wellness Plan suggests for you a disciplined regime. You need to begin by forgiving yourself your past mistakes.

Moderation in all things is your key to success: balanced nutrition, losing a few pounds, taking your antioxidant nutrients, such as B, C, and E vitamins. Scheduled work, rest and play, plus attuning yourself to the more spiritual aspects of life are your safeguards to health and longevity.

Your namesake, Bacchus, is the same as the name given to the first Roman Holiday, the most festive day of the year. You, a long-lived enthusiast who enjoys home-life, a popular man with your associates and peers, can let your playful spirit soar. All you have to do to have it all, is find that peace within yourself that surpasses understanding.

STRENGTHS AND WEAKNESSES

You are now typed as Bacchus, the mythical god who embodies these strengths:

- ✦ A natural communicator
- ✦ A charming and playful disposition
- ✦ Emotional security when relating to the opposite sex
- ✦ A motivation for independent achievement
- ✦ An innate ability to secure wealth
- ✦ A likable and cooperative personality
- ✦ Self-confident when competing

Bacchus' weaknesses are:

- ✦ An oversensitivity to parental shortcomings
- ✦ A susceptibility to disillusionment
- ✦ An inclination to acquire addictions
- ✦ When hurt, a tendency to be vindictive
- ✦ An innate desire to overindulge
- ✦ A self-defeatist attitude
- ✦ A super-sensitivity to environmental pollutants

Step II: Reprogramming Your Psyche

BACCHUS' AFFIRMATION

I acknowledge that in the past
I have not recognized my self-destructive ways
And my need for balance.
Realizing my shortcomings,
I pledge now to follow
My true life's purpose
And change my daily habits
To honor body, mind, and spirit as one.
I affirm to uphold this pledge,
Out of love for myself,
And for all fellow human beings.

INCENSE

Rose, lavender, musk, pine, sandalwood

CANDLES

Orange: for temperance
Green: for fostering forgiveness
White: for higher awareness

Step III: Creating Healthy Nutrition

Refer to Chapter VII, Pages 266 – 285.

Step IV: Color Support in the Wardrobe

BACCHUS' PALETTE COLORS

Supporting Colors

Balancers	Securers	Inspirers	Protectors
Wine	Grape	Mauve	Black
Dark brown	Cherry red	Rose beige	Brick red
Gold	Honey	Tan	Khaki
Wheat	Lemon yellow	Cream	Pine
Olive green	Apple green	Celery	Leaf green
Slate blue	Sea green	Citrus yellow	Turquoise
Pewter gray	Bright blue	Wedgwood blue	Navy blue

Avoidance Colors

Bacchus needs to avoid all shades of orange, including pumpkin and rust. These colors stimulate a false sense of personal security and leave him inclined to excessive gratification of his appetites. Since orange is a mixture of both yellow and red, the color can drain the adrenal-root nerve reflex causing an excessive production of adrenaline.

Step V: Gem and Stone Strengthening

WELLNESS SUPPORT STONES FOR BACCHUS

For the Physical Body

- Coral (especially red) – supports sexual stamina
- Wood (petrified and agatized) – prevents energy depletion
- Jasper (all colors) – increases physical endurance
- Ivory, bone, fossil – strengthens structural system

For the Emotional System

- Pearls and mother-of-pearl – foster self-security
- Moonstone – encourages self-love
- Amber – protects from stress
- Tiger's eye – stabilizes the emotions

For Spiritual and Mental Awareness

- Amethyst – enhances intuition
- Jade – promotes objectivity
- Tourmaline – fosters inner peace
- Aventurine – increases insight and perception

Step VI: Scents, Herbal Elixirs, and Oils

BACCHUS' SCENTS, ELIXIRS, AND OILS

Bacchus' scents lift his spirits and calm his emotions, his elixirs help him to maintain his youthfulness, and his oils strengthen his immune system.

Scents	Elixirs	Oils
Lavender	Rose Water & Glycerin	Vitamin E
Rose	Apricot	Citrus
Musk	Milk and Honey	Almond
Sandalwood	Cocoa butter	Musk
Pine	Lanolin	Myrrh

Step VII: Hobbies and Interests

BACCHUS' PERSONALITY KEY

Bacchus likes to release tension through noncontact sports and activities, and he enjoys companionships. He should consider sports that foster partnership and self-confidence.

Outdoor

- ✧ Playing baseball and volleyball
- ✧ Horseback riding
- ✧ Skiing and tobogganing
- ✧ Taking family vacations
- ✧ Constructing and repairing house items and working in the yard
- ✧ Surf and stream fishing
- ✧ Snorkeling and scuba diving

Indoor

- ✧ Bowling
- ✧ Disco or ballroom dancing
- ✧ Taking photographs and studying photography
- ✧ Interior designing and sculpturing
- ✧ Playing racquetball
- ✧ Collecting stamps and antiques
- ✧ Reading short stories and newspapers

Step VIII: Exercises for Glandular Improvement

Bacchus' Exercise Routines

These exercises are meant to augment, not replace, your regular exercise routine. For further information, see the Recommended Reading section at the end of this book.

Bacchus' exercises have been divided into three categories: warm-ups, toning exercises, and deep relaxation, to be followed by an out-of-door exercise for improved circulation, such as short jogs, swimming, or bike riding.

1. Warm-ups: Overall spine stretches, torso twists to music (see Figure 15), arm raises and push-offs, knee to chest lifts, and feet and ankle stretches (for ten minutes).

2. Toning Exercises: Weight lifting, step aerobics or stair climbing, and Nautilus ski or rowing machine exercises (for ten minutes).

3. Deep Relaxation: From a seated position—spine straight , hands in lap—meditative relaxation to music while directing healing energy to head, midsection, and base of spine (for five to ten minutes).

Figure 15 • Standing Torso Twists

Step IX: Divine Relationships

BACCHUS' FEMALE COMPATIBILITY CHART

	EXCELLENT	VERY GOOD	GOOD	FAIR	POOR
ROMANCE	ATHENA	APHRODITE MINERVA	DIANA IRIS VENUS	ARTEMIS	
FRIENDSHIP		APHRODITE ATHENA	DIANA IRIS MINERVA VENUS	ARTEMIS	
WORK		APHRODITE ATHENA	IRIS MINERVA VENUS	ARTEMIS DIANA	

You, as a Bacchus, are often considered by women a knight in shining armor and you enjoy playing the role. Your first choice of female goddesses is Athena, quickly followed by Aphrodite and Minerva, as these women will appreciate your manliness or provide for you the nurturing you did not receive as a child.

Since you often bend the rules, your least likely choices in female companionship are the more conventional goddesses, Artemis and Diana. However, once you establish a home, you're seldom found in the divorce courts. You leave the philosophy of life to her and you manage the everyday world.

Bacchus, you are a god who likes variety in your male companions, choosing both the jocks and the sensitives simultaneously. You look up to the Mercurys and Neptunes as father figures for your enhancement, but prefer other Bacchuses, Atlases, Eroses, and Apollos for your social companionship. The older, wiser men stimulate your mind; however, you are keenly aware that you can only be up in your head for so long, and then you must get grounded. Your long-term friendships are with gods who consider you both a well-rounded person and a plus to their social commitments, family or otherwise.

Step X: The Inner Power – Meditation

Meditation Exercise

To meditate you should follow these seven basic steps:

1. Find a quiet area or corner of a room where you will not be disturbed. Near you, place a favorite religious or spiritual object, such as a statue, a crystal, or a mandala.

2. Sit on a straight-backed chair with your feet firmly planted on the floor, or sit cross-legged on the floor with your spine erect.

3. Relax your neck by rotating it, first to the right and then to the left. Tense your shoulders up; then let them fall and relax.

4. Take several deep cleansing breaths and, as you fully exhale the last one, you feel your tension leave.

5. Concentrate on a mantra (a prayer, chant, or hymn) or a monosyllabic word, such as OM.

6. Remain still for ten to fifteen minutes while attempting to control your thoughts, letting your spiritual nature nourish you.

7. Open your eyes, and come slowly back to conscious awareness. Take another deep breath, and feel yourself enveloped in the healing flow. Now you are ready to return to your outer world, feeling renewed and regenerated from the power within.

Deep Relaxation

For deep relaxation, follow these five steps:

1. No particular space is needed for this practice, just yourself.

2. Lift your head up, stick out your chin and tense your neck; then drop your head toward your chest thinking, "I relax my head and I release my mind from all tension."

3. Continue down your body in the same manner—neck, shoulders (tense, then relax); chest, arms, hands (tense, then relax); abdomen, hips, thighs (tense, then relax); and finally, legs, calves, ankles, and feet—releasing all parts of the body from tension.

4. Breathe quietly and rhythmically, feeling the healing energy flow throughout your body.

5. Now, mentally send healing to any part of your body that still feels tense, knowing that health and happiness are yours to claim.

ATLAS

The Community Father

Step I: Understanding Your Personality

The mythical Atlas, a Greek god, was the son of a Titan giant and a water nymph, and the brother of Prometheus, the creator of humankind. He was believed to be the protector of the columns that divided heaven from earth. In punishment for warring with Zeus, the king of the gods, he was condemned to support the entire earth on his shoulders.

The Creative Wellness Atlas is a natural pillar of the community. He has a strong sense of civic leadership and responsibility, but tends to overwork himself.

If you have been typed as an Atlas, you are a good family man, a hard worker, and a responsible citizen. You continually better yourself intellectually and professionally. You strive for success and financial independence. You prefer to live a conventional life with a home, family, and stable job, because above all else you want to feel secure and loved. Although you are for the most part forthright and straightforward with others, you often hide your feelings from yourself until you are in danger of losing your own identity.

As an Atlas, you usually take an active part in civic and community affairs in which you can express your talents and better your social status. Choosing a secure livelihood, partly because your parents didn't have the same opportunities you've had, you have wanted success from very early in your life. Your father probably had more influence on you, positively or negatively, than did your mother. Consequently, you continually try to prove yourself a worthy son.

You, an Atlas, love to work with your hands and your mind, from computers to all things mechanical. You are a natural coach and teacher, and enjoy hiking with the Boy Scouts or heading a National Football League team. You can be as detailed as an accountant or run the local grocery store. Importantly, your versatility in career choice is exceeded by none.

Recognizable men who portray the Atlas archetype are the former coach of the Washington Redskins, Joe Gibbs; Sam Walton, head of Wal-Mart Stores; Senator Jack Kemp, former head of HUD; and J. Irving Weiss (publisher/bank researcher). These men show how versatile the Atlas personality can be in the job market.

The Atlas man can blame his early upbringing as the major cause for his inability to express his feelings. He feels deeply, but because he fears social reprisals, he remains quiet to his own opinions. Many of you great men may have had hero worship as a youngster, and are role models as Big Brothers to the youth today. However, placing your hero outside of yourself may have created a negative effect as well, for you have had to live up to your heroic ideals or suffer feelings of inadequacy, worry, or guilt.

Your relationships with women are usually quite satisfactory if you can lead. Since you are a man's man, you like your woman in the home or in a noncompetitive field to yours. Due to social pressures, you will normally not be found in the divorce courts, for you will seek counseling first.

Your physical problems are usually caused by the ineffectual way you handle stress. You were never taught as a child to trust your feelings and, since you are more sensitive than you give yourself credit for being, you internalize your day-to-day stresses. Compounded, these can create anxieties that alter the alkaline/acid ratio in your blood chemistry, making you digestive sensitive. Genetically, you may have pancreatic history in your family, and if you become overweight, you must watch your blood sugar levels as well. Some symptoms of these digestive disturbances are loss of concentration, overall weakness, and pains in your abdomen. If these become severe, it's time to see your physician.

The Creative Wellness Plan fosters good health for you, Atlas. You begin with self-introspection and self-acceptance. You then apply your responsibility and your concern for others to yourself. You choose the right foods in your diet, you exercise, you involve yourself in hobbies that will reward you with the love you deserve, such as, taking a long-awaited cruise or learning to square-dance with your partner.

It isn't necessary that you, like Atlas the god, hold the whole world on your shoulders. Make peace with your inner father/mother god, thereby turning yourself over to the highest authority to free you of unnecessary self-imposed duty consciousness. This will give you the opportunity to share your true nature with others, the Community Father.

STRENGTHS AND WEAKNESSES

You are now typed as Atlas, the mythical god who embodies these strengths:

 ✧ Dedication to family and community

 ✧ Capable of shouldering responsibility

 ✧ Professional competence

 ✧ Ability to nurture and support others

 ✧ Astute intellect

 ✧ Innate drive for success

 ✧ All-around versatility

Atlas' weaknesses are:

 ✧ Feelings of inadequacy

 ✧ Lacks self-confidence due to low self-esteem

 ✧ Repressed emotional nature

 ✧ A tendency to overburden himself

 ✧ A disregard of his physical needs

 ✧ An inclination to worry unnecessarily

 ✧ A guilt-ridden conscience

Step II: Reprogramming Your Psyche

ATLAS' AFFIRMATION

I acknowledge that in the past
I have disregarded my emotional
And physical needs for balance.
Realizing my shortcomings,
I therefore pledge
To transform these habits.
I affirm to honor my true nature
And become an integrated person,
Mind, body, and spirit as one,
Bringing me balance and love,
And the ability to share it with others.

INCENSE

Frangipani, orange blossom, carnation, sandalwood, and strawberry

CANDLES

Orange:	for more faith in self
Lavender:	for peace of mind
White:	for higher awareness

Step III: Creating Healthy Nutrition

Refer to Chapter VIII, Pages 308 – 329.

Step IV: Color Support in the Wardrobe

ATLAS' PALETTE COLORS

Supporting Colors

Balancers	Securers	Inspirers	Protectors
Saddle brown	Chinese red	Shrimp	Burgundy
Rust	Pumpkin	Peach	Sienna brown
Khaki	Gold	Champagne	Sunshine yellow
Evergreen	Lemon	Celery	Wheat
Navy blue	Nile green	Mint	Apple green
Midnight blue	Turquoise	Sky blue	Pine
Black	Royal blue	Silver	Felt gray

Avoidance Colors

Atlas needs to avoid all shades of purple, including lavender and plum, since he uses these colors to hide his feelings of being overburdened by responsibilities. Repressed emotions cause him digestive disturbances and the color purple enforces his control of the same emotions.

Step V: Gem and Stone Strengthening

WELLNESS SUPPORT STONES FOR ATLAS

For the Physical Body

- Carnelian – stabilizes blood sugar levels
- Bloodstone and green Jasper – promote good circulation

- Wood (petrified and agatized) – provides physical endurance
- Jasper (all colors) – increases energy levels

For the Emotional System

- Blue lace agate – promotes tranquillity
- Sodalite – relieves an overactive conscience
- Mother-of-pearl – increases self-worth
- Tiger's eye – prevents overextending self

For Spiritual and Mental Awareness

- Jade (especially green) – helps develop wisdom
- Turquoise – gives tranquillity and insight
- Crystal – enhances healing abilities
- Moonstone – increases inner faith

Step VI: Scents, Herbal Elixirs, and Oils

ATLAS' SCENTS, ELIXIRS, AND OILS

Atlas' scents help him to release stress and lift his spirits, his elixirs aid the pH balance of his skin, and his oils support cellular rejuvenation.

Scents	Elixirs	Oils
Frangipani	Herbal Mixtures	Jojoba
Orange blossom	Cucumber	Wheat germ
Sandalwood	Chamomile	Lemon/Lime
Carnation	Aloe	Mink
Strawberry	Oatmeal	Lanolin

Step VII: Hobbies and Interests

ATLAS' PERSONALITY KEY

Atlas loves basic and practical entertainment and home activities. He should consider hobbies that build his confidence and allow him to be appreciated by other people.

Outdoor

- ✦ Farming
- ✦ Camping
- ✦ Going to amusement parks
- ✦ Bike riding
- ✦ Playing softball
- ✦ Taking family vacations
- ✦ Constructing and repairing around the house and working in the yard

Indoor

- ✦ Body building
- ✦ Square dancing and country dancing
- ✦ Gourmet cooking
- ✦ Making pottery
- ✦ Coaching and other "big brother" activities
- ✦ Bowling
- ✦ Fish breeding and caring for aquariums

Step VIII: *Exercises for Glandular Improvement*
Atlas' Exercise Routines

These exercises are meant to augment, not replace, your regular exercise routine. For further information , see the Recommended Reading section at the end of this book.

Atlas' exercises have been divided into four categories: warm-ups, toning exercise, Yoga disciplines, and relaxation for improved digestion and metabolism. You, an Atlas, enjoy being supported during an exercise regime; so become a member of a health club or a body-building center and it will improve your image and health.

1. Warm-ups: At home, bend and stretch exercises upon arising, followed by jumping jacks (five minutes).

2. Toning exercises: Modified sit-ups, torso stretches and twists, hip and leg raises, and push-ups (four positions of 2 ½ minutes each).

3. Yoga disciplines: Yoga knee-to-chest pose (see Figure 16), followed by the Yoga spinal twist and the Yoga bow pose (for two minutes each).

4. Relaxation: Prone breathing meditative exercises to music while directing the healing energy to the midsection of the body (for ten minutes).

Figure 16 • *Yoga Knee-to-Chest Pose*

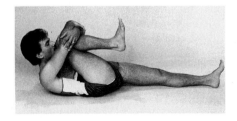

Step IX: Divine Relationships

ATLAS' COMPATIBILITY CHART

	EXCELLENT	VERY GOOD	GOOD	FAIR	POOR
ROMANCE	ARTEMIS	DIANA MINERVA	APHRODITE IRIS VENUS	ATHENA	
FRIENDSHIP		ARTEMIS DIANA MINERVA	APHRODITE VENUS	ATHENA IRIS	
WORK	ARTEMIS	DIANA MINERVA	IRIS VENUS	APHRODITE ATHENA	

You, as an Atlas, seek in romance, friendship, and work, the stable, conventional, yet sexual female. The goddesses that turn you on are Artemis, Diana, and Minerva. Not only do these women have similar interests to you, but they will stand by your side in most every undertaking.

Goddesses that are hard to domesticate are not to your liking, as you like to be the boss at home. Atlas, the community father, seldom marries until he has found the right woman because he feels responsible to tradition and community life. Women enjoy your maturity and wish that everyone could have you as the "Big Daddy."

Atlas, you choose different male friends, depending upon your interests. Some of you keep your working associates in one group and your playing buddies in another, for you like to keep your work separated from your play. You respect the talents of Mercury and Hermes when it comes to expertise on the job, but you like to socialize with Eros, Bacchus, and another Atlas, as these types provide the emotional opportunities for you to let down your resolve. Sometimes you play hard and need the skilled Apollo on your side; however, when the game is over, you both go your separate ways.

Step X: The Inner Power – Meditation

Meditation Exercise

To meditate you should follow these seven basic steps:

1. Find a quiet area or corner of a room where you will not be disturbed. Near you, place a favorite religious or spiritual object, such as a statue, a crystal, or a mandala.

2. Sit on a straight-backed chair with your feet firmly planted on the floor, or sit cross-legged on the floor with your spine erect.

3. Relax your neck by rotating it, first to the right and then to the left. Tense your shoulders up; then let them fall and relax.

4. Take several deep cleansing breaths and, as you fully exhale the last one, you feel your tension leave.

5. Concentrate on a mantra (a prayer, chant, or hymn) or a monosyllabic word, such as OM.

6. Remain still for ten to fifteen minutes while attempting to control your thoughts, letting your spiritual nature nourish you.

7. Open your eyes, and come slowly back to conscious awareness. Take another deep breath, and feel yourself enveloped in the healing flow. Now you are ready to return to your outer world, feeling renewed and regenerated from the power within.

Deep Relaxation

For deep relaxation, follow these five steps:

1. No particular space is needed for this practice, just yourself.

2. Lift your head up, stick out your chin and tense your neck; then drop your head toward your chest thinking, "I relax my head and I release my mind from all tension."

3. Continue down your body in the same manner—neck, shoulders (tense, then relax); chest, arms, hands (tense, then relax); abdomen, hips, thighs (tense, then relax); and finally, legs, calves, ankles, and feet—releasing all parts of the body from tension.

4. Breathe quietly and rhythmically, feeling the healing energy flow throughout your body.

5. Now, mentally send healing to any part of your body that still feels tense, knowing that health and happiness are yours to claim.

EROS

The Creative Builder

Step I: Understanding Your Personality

The mythical Eros, son of Aphrodite, was the winged Greek god of love and sexual potency, but as a child was often mischievous. An agent for the continuation of life, he brought couples together to build and increase the seeds of humanity. However, his passion for power caused him to break law and order, many times destroying what he had built.

The Creative Wellness Eros is a natural builder with a quick mind, a love for women, and many talents in the arts. Unfortunately, his self-destructive inclinations can damage him physically and emotionally.

If you have been typed as an Eros, you are a contemporary man, a man of the times—intelligent, sensitive, and romantic. You usually look younger than your years, and you portray this youthfulness in your lifestyle and habits. You love athletics, appreciate the body, and enjoy the companionship of both men and women.

Everyone loves an Eros. You can overcome your innate lack of self-assurance by making yourself admired by your winning wit and charm. In addition, you have exceptional artistic talents, and some of you will choose a career in either music, acting, or the visual arts. Though you may not realize it, you are also a natural builder, manager, and healer. These abilities, along with your superb manual dexterity, should ensure that you never find yourself without work. You are a person who can survive under any circumstances, often holding two jobs simultaneously, and you can achieve almost any goal you set out to accomplish.

Renowned men who image the archetypal Eros are Steven Spielberg, Michael Jackson, Donald Trump, and Billy Graham. These men personify the versatility of the Eros personality—the director, the singer and dancer, the builder, and the evangelist.

As an Eros, you have a primary weakness, an emotional insecurity stemming from your childhood, which can sometimes undermines your success. Most likely it developed in your early years, when one of your parents, probably your father, disappointed you. To compensate for what you considered his failings and to appear as manly as possible, you repressed your feelings of disillusionment, or sought some form of escape. Along with the frustration you felt at not being able to change your situation, you were left with the potential for depression and anxieties. The emotional turmoil may also have triggered your inherent pancreatic enzyme vulnerability, affecting your digestive system, causing allergies, and severe stress-related illnesses, such as colitis and ulcers. However, no one would guess the turmoil inside yourself. A master at hiding your feelings, the born actor, you appear to the world as the calmest, most controlled of men. Those who don't know you well might say you wear a mask of indifference or aloofness. Some of you habitually overindulge in emotional pacifiers— sugar, chocolate, alcohol, or drugs. Under your cool exterior, more than any other god, your physical health can suffer from your need to escape. You therefore must always pay close attention to your health maintenance and balance.

In the department of women, you never should worry, for you have an abundance of sex appeal. You appreciate beautiful, intelligent, liberated damsels, but you don't want to rescue them—in fact, quite the opposite. You might like them to rescue you! You usually choose mates that have your mother's characteristics and are often accused of being a "mama's boy." In truth, this is not a co-dependency, but rather an inherent trait that you appreciate and respect your mother.

The Creative Wellness Plan suggests for an Eros that he moderate himself in all that he does, and that he seek the spiritual side of himself to bring the calm he so badly wants. By counseling sessions or support groups, he can discover his true feelings and how to express them more fully. He can rescue the sensitive little boy within that's been hurt, and become more at peace with his own mature masculinity. Another step toward wellness and longevity is preventative health maintenance: good, balanced nutrition for his body, natural supports for his emotional needs, and hobbies for his creative outlets.

Mr. Romantic can build the highest building, climb Mt. Everest, and become a renowned artist all in a single lifetime. He is the envy of all the other gods and will never become spoiled by adulation from all the goddesses. He can become a spiritual way-shower and transformer in any community and assure by his example the continuity of all life for the future.

STRENGTHS AND WEAKNESSES

You are now typed as Eros, the mythical god who embodies these strengths:

- ✧ Innate artistic talent
- ✧ Idealistic and romantic inclinations
- ✧ Instinctive survival capabilities
- ✧ Sensitivity to the needs of women
- ✧ A dedication to work
- ✧ An ability to learn and adapt quickly
- ✧ Natural manual dexterity

Eros' weaknesses are:

- ✧ Innate feelings of emotional insecurity
- ✧ Disillusionment with the father figure
- ✧ Resists authority controls
- ✧ A tendency to escapism
- ✧ Self-destructive habits
- ✧ Frequently immature
- ✧ Resents female domination

Step II: Reprogramming Your Psyche

EROS' AFFIRMATION

I acknowledge that in the past
I have disregarded my physical
And emotional needs
Which have caused me undue stress.
I therefore pledge
To seek higher understanding
So that I might change my habits
And become a more integrated person,
Body, mind, and soul as one.
I now accept the spiritual purpose for my existence
And pledge to live it,
To the best of my abilities
In all that I do.

INCENSE

Sandalwood, jasmine, lavender, pine or juniper, lemon/lime

CANDLES

Orange: for emotional security
Light blue: for calming anxiety
White: for higher awareness

Step III: Creating Healthy Nutrition

Refer to Chapter VIII, Pages 308 – 329.

Step IV: Color Support in the Wardrobe

EROS' PALETTE COLORS

Supporting Colors

Balancers	Securers	Inspirers	Protectors
Dark brown	Plum	Shrimp	Brick red
Burgundy	Scarlet	Rose beige	Chinese red
Sienna brown	Melon	Tan	Gold
Rust	Sunshine yellow	Champagne	Khaki
Honey	Citrus yellow	Celery	Leaf green
Pine	Nile green	Mint	Emerald
Pewter gray	Midnight blue	Mauve	Charcoal gray

Avoidance Colors

Eros needs to avoid all shades of light to medium blues, as these shades tend to overstimulate his mind, causing him to disregard his physical and emotional sensitivities. The lighter blues do not support the digestive process, thus undermining his energy and stamina.

Step V: Gem and Stone Strengthening

WELLNESS SUPPORT STONES FOR EROS

For the Physical Body

- Carnelian – stabilizes pancreatic function
- Dendrite and speckled agate – protect against injury
- Jasper (all colors) – increases energy levels
- Corals and shells – gives physical endurance

For the Emotional System

- Mother-of-pearl – provides emotional security
- Black onyx – prevents overreaction to stress
- Turquoise – alleviates anxiety
- Amber – protects sensitive nature

For Spiritual and Mental Awareness

- Tiger's eye – stimulates clear discernment
- Jade – fosters wisdom
- Aquamarine – inspires creativity
- Crystal – helps develop communication skills

Step VI: Scents, Herbal Elixirs, and Oils

EROS' SCENTS, ELIXIRS, AND OILS

Eros' scents help to support his sensitivities, his elixirs aid his natural immunity, and his oils calm his nervous system and prevent aging.

Scents	Elixirs	Oils
Jasmine	Aloe	Almond
Sandalwood	Cucumber	Rose Oil
Lavender	Vitamin A & D	Pine
Pine	Herbal Mixtures	Musk
Lemon/Lime	Lanolin	Citrus

Step VII: Hobbies and Interests

EROS' PERSONALITY KEY

Eros enjoys projects that both involve construction and require working with people. He should consider activities that build his self-esteem and require manual dexterity.

Outdoor

- ✧ Playing baseball
- ✧ Stream fishing
- ✧ Taking weekend vacations
- ✧ Rockhounding
- ✧ Caring for animals
- ✧ Archery
- ✧ Gardening and landscaping

Indoor

- ✧ Repairing household items
- ✧ Participating in fitness and health programs
- ✧ Playing raquetball
- ✧ Making home movies and videos
- ✧ Bowling
- ✧ Painting and wood carving
- ✧ Playing darts and billiards

Step VIII: Exercises for Glandular Improvement

Eros' Exercise Routines

These exercises are meant to augment, not replace, your regular exercise routine. For further information , see the Recommended Reading section at the end of this book.

Eros' exercises have been divided into four categories: warm-ups, stamina boosters, spinal flexors, and relaxation for improved autoimmune functions and digestive enzyme performance. You, an Eros, are both active and sport conscious, so become a member of a team, enjoy a tennis or racquet club, or a body-building center.

1. Warm-ups: At home, stretch and bend exercises upon arising, followed by feet and ankle flexing and jumping jacks (five minutes).

2. Stamina boosters: Push-ups, sit-ups, chest openers with light weights, and head to knee bends (four positions of $2\frac{1}{2}$ minutes each).

3. Spinal flexibility: Seated spinal twists, kneeling torso stretchers (see Figure 17), and lateral leg lifts (for two minutes each).

4. Relaxation: Prone breathing meditative exercises to music, while directing the healing energy to the midsection of the body (for ten minutes).

Figure 17 • Kneeling Torso Stretcher

Step IX: Divine Relationships

EROS' FEMALE COMPATIBILITY CHART

	EXCELLENT	VERY GOOD	GOOD	FAIR	POOR
ROMANCE	VENUS	APHRODITE ATHENA	IRIS DIANA	ARTEMIS MINERVA	
FRIENDSHIP		APHRODITE ATHENA VENUS	ARTEMIS DIANA IRIS MINERVA	DIANA	
WORK		APHRODITE ARTEMIS	ATHENA DIANA MINERVA VENUS	IRIS	

You, as an Eros, are the god of romance and bring out the dream nature in the goddesses. Venus, Aphrodite your opposite, and Athena, are your best choices for romance and friendship, as their free spirit and independence bring out the best in you.

Some of you have the privilege of working with an Artemis who considers you an equal, although in reality she may be your boss. Many of you have more than one marriage, but you're always willing to try again because you love having a mate. A stress-free relationship with any of the goddesses is one where your sensitivities are understood and you as a man are appreciated.

Eros, you prefer the thyroid types of Apollo and Mercury in most professional relationships for you want to be supported by those "in the know." Like Bacchus, you choose your male buddies to support your need for emotional self-expression and physical competence, such as Bacchus, Atlas, and Eros. Your patron or counselor could be a Neptune or Hermes, but you do not wish to socialize with him because you don't like to be put in a compromising position. You create long-term friendships only with those who appreciate you and who contribute to the relationship. These men never need question your loyalty in return.

Step X: The Inner Power – Meditation

Meditation Exercise

To meditate you should follow these seven basic steps:

1. Find a quiet area or corner of a room where you will not be disturbed. Near you, place a favorite religious or spiritual object, such as a statue, a crystal, or a mandala.

2. Sit on a straight-backed chair with your feet firmly planted on the floor, or sit cross-legged on the floor with your spine erect.

3. Relax your neck by rotating it, first to the right and then to the left. Tense your shoulders up; then let them fall and relax.

4. Take several deep cleansing breaths and, as you fully exhale the last one, you feel your tension leave.

5. Concentrate on a mantra (a prayer, chant, or hymn) or a monosyllabic word, such as OM.

6. Remain still for ten to fifteen minutes while attempting to control your thoughts, letting your spiritual nature nourish you.

7. Open your eyes, and come slowly back to conscious awareness. Take another deep breath, and feel yourself enveloped in the healing flow. Now you are ready to return to your outer world, feeling renewed and regenerated from the power within.

Deep Relaxation

For deep relaxation, follow these five steps:

1. No particular space is needed for this practice, just yourself.

2. Lift your head up, stick out your chin, and tense your neck; then drop your head toward your chest thinking, "I relax my head and I release my mind from all tension."

3. Continue down your body in the same manner—neck, shoulders (tense, then relax); chest, arms, hands (tense, then relax); abdomen, hips, thighs (tense, then relax); and finally, legs, calves, ankles, and feet—releasing all parts of the body from tension.

4. Breathe quietly and rhythmically, feeling the healing energy flow throughout your body.

5. Now, mentally send healing to any part of your body that still feels tense, knowing that health and happiness are yours to claim.

HERMES

The Community Guardian

Step I: Understanding Your Personality

The mythical Hermes, son of Zeus, was a swift and graceful messenger for the gods. He was the patron of music, art, and various forms of divination. Eloquent and shrewd by nature, he was often represented as a pastoral character guarding his flock, as a shepherd would sheep. His staff with two serpents entwined is the symbol of the medical profession today.

The Creative Wellness Hermes is a natural healer and community supporter. One would find him in the medical arts, in community services, in law-and-order professions, and in other life-sustaining enterprises, such as insurance and real estate. However, his low self-esteem can cause emotional and mental conflicts, undermining his capabilities.

If you have been typed as a Hermes, you are a man of many talents. You are intellectually astute, quick-witted, glib, and often too generous. You like to hide your feelings behind a mask of indifference so others don't intrude upon your private life. This facade is not always successful, though, since the intensity of your personality shows through your penetrating eyes. You make a wonderful physician, since you are generous with your time and concern.

Nor do you have any trouble establishing a family or home. You are obsessed with social etiquette, as you like to be respected and rewarded in all aspects of life by colleagues, relatives, and community. You honor women, but you do not like to compete with them professionally, for you basically like a "man's world." You can be found on the golf course, in fraternity clubs, and in the priesthood. Recognizable men who portray the archetypal Hermes are Reverend Robert Schuller, Supreme Court Justice Clarence Thomas, Dr. Tim Johnson ("Good Morning America"), and Governor Mario Cuomo of New York State. These men exhibit some of the top positions in their

℃

fields of humanitarian service—the spiritual teacher, the judge, the inform-
ing doctor, and the "for-the-people" representative.

As a Hermes, your biggest weakness is your inner conflict born out of
a need for love and reward. You put yourself out for others and expect to
have them do the same for you. If this doesn't happen, you become easily
discouraged and can lose your self-esteem, or can even become resentful
and blaming. In extreme cases, you may deal with your excessive emotional needs by developing a neurosis or choosing a reclusive existence.
Having your survival threatened as a child, either because of illness or lack
of family financial security, is one of the reasons for these ungrounded
fears. In adulthood, this explains why many Hermes have a strong drive
to succeed and overserve the less fortunate of the community. You, or
they, can empathize with their problems.

Since most emotional problems affect the midsection of the body and
all the organs contained within, you Hermes, are no exception. Your potential weakness is centered in your pancreas and liver. Since the pancreas and
liver working together ensure that nutrients are properly processed for cellular
rejuvenation, their malfunction during times of stress can adversely affect
overall digestion. Any number of serious illnesses can be the result, particularly after age 40.

The Creative Wellness Plan suggests that all Hermes watch what they
eat. Chemicals and additives are detrimental to you especially, as these
agents interfere with proper liver performance. It is important that you
know your nutritional needs and stay with a pure balance diet. High-fat
and gourmet foods are not the best for you. To keep yourself discomfort-
and symptom-free, you require healthy out-of-doors exercise, natural supports
to protect your sensitive emotional system, and plenty of rest, relaxation,
and play.

Since you are character-strong and capable of overcoming almost any
obstacle you encounter at work or at home, you more than any of the other
gods possess a talent for transformation. You have a knack for increasing

wealth, securing your family, supporting community improvement, and leading a comfortable self-fulfilled existence. With this resourcefulness and generosity, you, as a Hermes, can give much to the world and aid its continued survival. Aren't you the messenger of the gods?

STRENGTHS AND WEAKNESSES

You are now typed as Hermes, the mythical god who embodies these strengths:

- ✧ Above-average intellectual capabilities
- ✧ A tenacious drive to achieve
- ✧ A natural inclination toward the healing arts
- ✧ Capability to provide for others
- ✧ A generous and considerate nature
- ✧ Sound financial judgment
- ✧ A humanitarian guardian

Hermes' weaknesses are:

- ✧ Low self-esteem
- ✧ Insecurities and survival neuroses
- ✧ Resentful and critical of others
- ✧ A tendency to become a recluse
- ✧ Excessive need for reward
- ✧ Frailty in health after 40
- ✧ Aloof and indifferent attitudes

Step II: Reprogramming Your Psyche

HERMES' AFFIRMATION

I acknowledge that in the past
I have overemphasized
My needs for security and reward.
In understanding my inner motivation,
I pledge to change myself,
And become an integrated person,
Body, mind, and spirit as one.
I forgive myself and others
Who have not recognized my worth,
So as to secure my future,
In health, love, and my pursuit of happiness.

INCENSE

Honeysuckle, sandalwood, gardenia, herbal, and pine

CANDLES

Orange:	for self-esteem
Red:	for positive attitude
Lime or pine green:	for self-healing

Step III: Creating Healthy Nutrition

Refer to Chapter VIII, Pages 308 – 329.

Step IV: Color Support in the Wardrobe

HERMES' PALETTE COLORS

Supporting Colors

Balancers	Securers	Inspirers	Protectors
Burgundy	Scarlet red	Shrimp	Sienna brown
Saddle brown	Honey	Rose beige	Chinese red
Rust	Lemon yellow	Tan	Cream
Gold	Champagne	Oyster	Turquoise
Wheat	Sea green	Mint	Navy blue
French gray	Bright blue	Eggshell blue	Plum
Slate blue	Purple	Lilac	Charcoal gray

Avoidance Colors

Hermes needs to avoid all jungle greens, such as shades of khaki to olive. These colors irritate the pancreas/liver nerve reflexes and can upset the digestive system, as well as cause emotional distress.

Step V: Gem and Stone Strengthening

WELLNESS SUPPORT STONES FOR HERMES

For the Physical Body

- Sards and carnelian – aid pancreatic performance
- Moss agate (all colors) – purifies the blood
- Jasper (all colors) – increases energy levels
- Wood (petrified and agatized) – stabilizes physical energy

For the Emotional System

- Mother-of-pearl – increases self-esteem
- Sodalite – dispels guilt
- Blue lace agate – alleviates anxiety
- Tiger's eye – fosters self-security

For Spiritual and Mental Awareness

- Turquoise – gives peace of mind
- Jade (all colors) – fosters wisdom
- Crystal – enhances healing abilities
- Lapis lazuli – expands mental faculties

Step VI: Scents, Herbal Elixirs, and Oils

HERMES' SCENTS, ELIXIRS, AND OILS

Hermes' scents help him to relax his mind, his elixirs support overall rejuvenation, and his oils improve circulation and his natural immunity.

Scents	Elixirs	Oils
Honeysuckle	Aloe	Olive
Sandalwood	Myrrh	Mineral
Pine	Vitamins A & D	Jasmine
Gardenia	Papaya	Jojoba
Herbal	Cucumber	Myrrh

Step VII: Hobbies and Interests

HERMES' PERSONALITY KEY

Hermes prefers mental pursuits to physical competition. He should consider activities that require quick thinking and coordination and build his sense of self-worth.

Outdoor

- ✧ Bay fishing
- ✧ Rock and gem collecting
- ✧ Camping
- ✧ Helping in wildlife conservation
- ✧ Bike riding
- ✧ Taking short trips
- ✧ Golfing

Indoor

- ✧ Collecting valuable artwork
- ✧ Playing computer games
- ✧ Playing ping-pong
- ✧ Speculating in the stock market
- ✧ Playing musical instruments – wind or string
- ✧ Studying esoteric ideas
- ✧ Joining a health and fitness club

Step VIII: Exercises for Glandular Improvement

Hermes' Exercise Routines

These exercises are meant to augment, not replace, your regular exercise routine. For further information , see the Recommended Reading section at the end of this book.

Hermes' exercises have been divided into four categories: warm-ups, toning exercises, spinal flexors, and relaxation for improved liver function and release of tension. You, a Hermes, are an extremely busy individual with little time for a disciplined regime, so these exercises are designed to keep you relaxed and healthy.

1. Warm-ups: At home, overall body stretches upon arising, and short walk or jog while deep-breathing fresh air (five minutes).

2. Toning exercises: Ten sit-ups, ten push-ups, and ten leg raises (ten minutes).

3. Spinal Flexibility: Knee to chest hugs, floor-seated spinal twists (see Figure 18), kneeling torso stretchers, and belly tucks (for ten minutes).

4. Relaxation: Guided meditation to music directing the healing energy to the midsection of the body (for five minutes).

Figure 18 • Seated Spinal Twist

Step IX: Divine Relationships

HERMES' FEMALE COMPATIBILITY CHART

	EXCELLENT	VERY GOOD	GOOD	FAIR	POOR
ROMANCE	MINERVA	ARTEMIS	APHRODITE DIANA	IRIS VENUS	ATHENA
FRIENDSHIP		ARTEMIS MINERVA	APHRODITE DIANA	IRIS VENUS	ATHENA
WORK		ARTEMIS MINERVA	APHRODITE DIANA VENUS	ATHENA IRIS	

You, a Hermes, are the greatest of partners or team players with either a Minerva or an Artemis. These women give you emotional satisfaction in your home or at work. Since your generosity supports the lifestyle of most of the Pancreas goddesses, you can choose which one suits you the best by kindred soul attraction.

Your insecurities are triggered by aggressive, competitive women and you will put distance between them and yourself emotionally, placing your energy elsewhere. The goddesses who win your heart are those who honor and respect you, and in turn, these are the lucky ones for you Hermes; give to them all that the world can provide.

Hermes, if the male relationship is of your choosing, you are a great partner or team builder. These same principles apply at either work or play, for you usually put your heart into your endeavor. You admire the gods like yourself, such as Mercury, Atlas, and another Hermes who feels loyalty in comradeship is above question. However, occasionally one of you may demonstrate a Machiavellian trait, putting your partner or friend in jeopardy without sensitivity to the consequences. Fortunately this only applies to segments of Hermes, as most of you do establish stable friendships with many of the gods and keep them that way.

Step X: The Inner Power – Meditation

Meditation Exercise

To meditate you should follow these seven basic steps:

1. Find a quiet area or corner of a room where you will not be disturbed. Near you, place a favorite religious or spiritual object, such as a statue, a crystal, or a mandala.

2. Sit on a straight-backed chair with your feet firmly planted on the floor, or sit cross-legged on the floor with your spine erect.

3. Relax your neck by rotating it, first to the right and then to the left. Tense your shoulders up; then let them fall and relax.

4. Take several deep cleansing breaths and, as you fully exhale the last one, you feel your tension leave.

5. Concentrate on a mantra (a prayer, chant, or hymn) or a monosyllabic word, such as OM.

6. Remain still for ten to fifteen minutes while attempting to control your thoughts, letting your spiritual nature nourish you.

7. Open your eyes, and come slowly back to conscious awareness. Take another deep breath, and feel yourself enveloped in the healing flow. Now you are ready to return to your outer world, feeling renewed and regenerated from the power within.

Deep Relaxation

For deep relaxation, follow these five steps:

1. No particular space is needed for this practice, just yourself.

2. Lift your head up, stick out your chin and tense your neck; then drop your head toward your chest thinking, "I relax my head and I release my mind from all tension."

3. Continue down your body in the same manner—neck, shoulders (tense, then relax); chest, arms, hands (tense, then relax); abdomen, hips, thighs (tense, then relax); and finally, legs, calves, ankles, and feet—releasing all parts of the body from tension.

4. Breathe quietly and rhythmically, feeling the healing energy flow throughout your body.

5. Now, mentally send healing to any part of your body that still feels tense, knowing that health and happiness are yours to claim.

PART III

CHAPTER VI:

NUTRITION PLANS
THYROID VULNERABILITLES

Balanced Nutrition Plan
for Athena and Artemis

Selective Diet: High Protein, Low Fat

Athena and Artemis fare best on diets high in protein and low in saturated fats. As long as they avoid junk foods that are fried or made with refined sugar or excessive salt, they can eat almost anything. However, they should limit their intake of alcohol and stimulants such as coffee, since these drinks give them little nutrition and also hinder the thyroid's regulation of their metabolism. For the extra energy they need because of their thyroid vulnerability, it is important that they include animal protein such as lean red meat or fresh fish in their daily diets.

Priority Foods

- Red meat: lean cuts of beef, veal, and lamb only
- Fresh fish: all kinds
- Fowl: all kinds but those mentioned in "Limited" and "Avoidance Foods" below
- Dairy: low-fat milk and cheese products only
- Vegetables: all kinds, especially green, at least three servings a day; include legumes for protein
- Grains and cereals: bulgur and whole-wheat, rye, bran, oats, brown rice
- Fruits: fresh daily
- Nuts and seeds: almonds, soy nuts, and sunflower and sesame seeds
- Oils: sunflower, sesame, safflower, and corn

Limited Foods

Pork, dark turkey meat, turkey and chicken skin, bleached white flour, raisins and highly sugared dried fruit, and beverages containing sugar and caffeine.

Avoidance Foods

Duck, processed meats, bacon, fried foods, ice cream, candies, pastries, chocolate, refined sugars, nitrates, MSG (monosodium glutamate), and alcohol (except light beer and wine).

Vitamin and Mineral Requirements

100 mg. B-complex, 1000 mg. vitamin C, and one or two 4-in-1 combination capsules (with vitamin B-6, kelp, lecithin, and apple cider vinegar) daily. Extra minerals like calcium or iron periodically.

Meal Timing

Three balanced meals, with occasional snacks. Avoid eating after 10:00 p.m., since your metabolism slows down then.

Morning meal . . . . .between 6:30 and 8:30 a.m.
Midmorning snack . . . . .between 10:30 and 11:30 a.m.
Midday meal . . . . .between noon and 2:00 p.m.
Midafternoon snack . . . . .between 2:30 and 3:30 p.m.
Evening meal . . . . .between 5:30 and 7:30 p.m.
Late snack . . . . .between 8:30 and 9:30 p.m.

Daily Instructions

- Drink at least six 8-ounce glasses of water daily.
- Never eat or drink as a substitute for emotional stress.
- Avoid midnight snacks whenever possible.
- Eat and drink slowly. Never eat when in a hurry.
- Enjoy experimenting with new health foods.

ATHENA & ARTEMIS
WEIGHT-MANAGEMENT CHART

Height (Without Shoes)	Desired Weight (Pounds) Small Frame	Medium Frame	Large Frame	Calorie Allowance for Maintained Weight
4' 10"	102 – 111	109 – 121	118 – 131	900 – 1000
11"	103 – 113	111 – 123	120 – 134	950 – 1100
5' 0"	104 – 115	113 – 126	122 – 137	1000 – 1200
1"	106 – 118	115 – 129	125 – 140	1050 – 1250
2"	108 – 121	118 – 132	128 – 143	1100 – 1300
3"	111 – 124	121 – 135	131 – 147	1150 – 1350
4"	114 – 127	124 – 138	134 – 151	1200 – 1400
5"	117 – 130	127 – 141	137 – 155	1250 – 1450
6"	120 – 133	130 – 144	140 – 159	1300 – 1500
7"	123 – 136	133 – 147	143 – 163	1350 – 1550
8"	126 – 139	136 – 150	146 – 167	1400 – 1600
9"	129 – 142	139 – 153	149 – 170	1450 – 1650
10"	132 – 145	142 – 156	152 – 173	1500 – 1700
11"	135 – 148	145 – 159	155 – 176	1550 – 1750
6' 0"	138 – 151	148 – 162	158 – 179	1600 – 1800

If you are an Athena or Artemis and want to know if you are the proper weight for your height and build, refer to the above weight-management chart. This chart is based on standard insurance companies' data (Society of Actuaries and Association of Life Insurance Medical Directors of America, 1984).

The calorie allowances are for ages twenty-five to fifty-nine. These ages represent most women in the United States today.

For those under twenty-five or over fifty-nine, the calorie allowances vary slightly from individual to individual. In general, more calories are needed in youth and fewer in the senior years, due to different lifestyle activities. (The calorie allowances indicated here are based on data from the N.I.H. National Institute on Aging, Baltimore, Maryland.)

SEVEN-DAY MENU PLAN
ATHENA & ARTEMIS

DAY 1 • WEIGHT LOSS
(*approximately 900 calories*)

Meal	Calories
BREAKFAST	
⅔ cup Wheatena	100
½ cup skim milk	45
5 sliced strawberries with	30
Teaspoon honey	20
Cup of decaffeinated coffee	—
	195
LUNCH	
1 slice of rye bread	75
4 ounces broiled extra lean ground beef patty	140
Broiled zucchini boat, sprinkled with paprika and dill weed	22
Salad with apple, orange, and pineapple slices on romaine lettuce	40
2 ounces skim milk cottage cheese	42
Iced herbal tea with lemon	—
	319

SNACK

Cup of Pero or hot herbal tea	
⅔ cup cucumber slices and broccoli flowerets	30
2 tablespoons plain yogurt with horseradish and chives dip	30
	60

DINNER

4 ounces of sliced roast turkey (light meat without skin)	200
½ cup steamed green beans, sprinkled with almond slivers	30
Salad of 4 artichoke hearts, ½ sliced tomato, chopped green onion, and watercress, with	45
Vinegar and 2 teaspoons oil dressing	80
Cup of hot herbal tea or Perrier with lime peel	—
	355

TOTAL CALORIES FOR THE DAY   929

DAY 2 • WEIGHT LOSS
(approximately 900 calories)

Meal	Calories

BREAKFAST

1 soft-boiled egg	80
1 Bran Muffin*	121
Cup of coffee	—
	201

*See recipe.

LUNCH

3 ounces thinly sliced roast leg of lamb	180
1 cup cut asparagus, steamed	33
1 slice sprouted wheat bread	65
Cup of hot water with lemon	—
	278

SNACK

6 ounces low-sodium V-8 juice	40
2 Rye-Krisp	42
	82

DINNER

4 ounces shellfish or 5 average shrimp (steamed, boiled, or baked)	100
Salad of cold artichoke heart, red cabbage, bibb lettuce, and green pepper rings, with	20
2 tablespoons apple cider vinegar and herb dressing	5
½ small acorn squash (baked)	75
¼ small cantaloupe	30
Cup of decaffeinated coffee	—
	230

SNACK

1 ounce skim milk cheese	70
2 Rye Melba Rounds	40
Perrier with lime	—
	110

TOTAL CALORIES FOR THE DAY   901

ᖆ

DAY 3 • WEIGHT LOSS
(approximately 1000 calories)

Meal	Calories
BREAKFAST	
½ cup All-Bran cereal	90
½ cup skim milk	45
½ cup blueberries	36
Cup of coffee, regular or decaffeinated	—
	171
SNACK	
1 cup raw vegetables (carrot sticks, celery sticks, cucumber slices)	40
½ cup skim milk cottage cheese	80
	120
LUNCH	
½ cup hot apple cider or apple juice	60
4 ounces broiled salmon steak	180
1 small baked potato	120
½ cup Chinese snow peas	30
Sautéed in 1 teaspoon sesame oil	42
1 slice pumpernickel bread	79
	511
DINNER	
4 ounces broiled chicken breast (remove skin)	150
½ cup steamed broccoli	20

Salad of alfalfa sprouts, shredded carrots, spinach, and scallions, with apple cider vinegar and herb dressing	38
	208

TOTAL CALORIES FOR THE DAY — 1010

DAY 4 • WEIGHT MAINTENANCE
(approximately 1000 calories)

Meal	Calories
BREAKFAST	
½ small grapefruit†	75
¾ cup wheat flakes	135
½ cup skim milk	45
Cup of coffee, regular or decaffeinated	—
	255
SNACK	
4 ounces low-sodium V-8 juice	25
2 Norwegian Flatbreads	40
	65

†Citrus eaten prior to (not after) dairy products will normally not cause digestive difficulty.

LUNCH	
6 ounces broiled sirloin steak	325
½ cup steamed broccoli	20
½ cup cooked black-eyed peas	70
1 slice rye bread	75
1 pat unsalted butter	36
Perrier with lemon slice	—
	526

DINNER

4 ounces baked fillet of flounder	80
1 cup Glazed Carrots*	30
Salad of alfalfa sprouts, bibb lettuce, scallions, and sliced cucumbers, with apple cider vinegar and dill	30
1 fresh peach	38
Cup of hot herbal tea with lemon	—
	178

TOTAL CALORIES FOR THE DAY   **1024**

DAY 5 • WEIGHT MAINTENANCE
(approximately 1200 calories)

Meal	Calories

BREAKFAST

1 soft poached egg on	80
½ slice whole-wheat toast	40
½ slice toast with 1 tablespoon Blueberry Jam*	50
4 ounces cranberry juice	82
	252

LUNCH

4 ounces thinly sliced roast beef	273
1 cup wax beans, steamed	33
1 Bran Muffin* with	121
1 pat of unsalted butter	33
Cup of decaffeinated coffee	—
	460

*See recipe.

SNACK

4 ounces low-fat fruit yogurt	125
3 Stoned Wheat Thins	38
	163

DINNER

Bowl of Fresh Broccoli Soup*	110
4 ounces crabmeat, steamed and chilled, on salad of cold artichoke heart	110
Spinach greens, and green pepper rings, with sliced beets and lemon	25
10 large sliced strawberries	37
2 Rye Melba Rounds	40
Glass of iced herbal tea	—
	322

TOTAL CALORIES FOR THE DAY   1197

DAY 6 • WEIGHT MAINTENANCE
(approximately 1200 calories)

Meal	Calories

BREAKFAST

⅔ cup oatmeal	100
½ cup skim milk	45
½ cup water-packed fruit cocktail	47
Cup of coffee	—
	192

SNACK

½ Bran Muffin* with 1 pat margarine	96
1 cup herbal tea	—
	96

*See recipe.

LUNCH

4 ounces broiled calves' liver	290
Salad with watercress, spinach leaves,	
alfalfa sprouts, and green onions, with	30
1 tablespoon low-calorie Italian oil	
and vinegar	18
½ cup boiled parslied potatoes (with skin)	60
½ cup brussels sprouts	28
Iced herbal tea	—
	426

SNACK

½ cup mixed cucumber slices, broccoli	
flowerets, and celery stalks	28
Cup of hot water with lemon	—
	28

DINNER

1 serving Lentil-Rice Stew*	155
Tossed Caesar salad with romaine lettuce,	
egg, garlic clove, mustard, and	
anchovies, garnished with	150
2 tablespoons whole-wheat bread crumbs	44
4-ounce glass of white Rhine wine	90
	439

TOTAL CALORIES FOR THE DAY   1181

*See recipe.

DAY 7 • FUN DAY
(approximately 1600 calories)

Meal	Calories

BREAKFAST

6 ounces cranberry juice cocktail	144
1 whole-wheat waffle	206
2 tablespoons maple syrup	100
Cup of coffee or Pero	—
	450

LUNCH

1 large slice Cauliflower Quiche*	270
Mixed green salad with hearts of palm,	
red pimentos, and capers	38
1 tablespoon French dressing	50
1 cup of Italian ice	125
1 almond cookie	35
Perrier with lime	—
	518

SNACK

1 oatmeal muffin with blueberries	130
1 cup herbal tea	—
	130

*See recipe.

∾

DINNER

1 skewer of lamb Shish Kabob*	300
½ cup long-grain brown rice	116
½ cup French-style green beans	16
1 Baked Apple with honey and cinnamon*	80
Cup of decaffeinated coffee or tea	—
	512

TOTAL CALORIES FOR THE DAY   **1610**

RECIPES FOR ATHENA & ARTEMIS' MEAL PLANNING

Athena's Fresh Broccoli Soup

2	pounds fresh broccoli, cleaned, trimmed, and cut into small pieces
2	cups water
2	cups chicken broth (natural stock or low-sodium canned)
1	teaspoon thyme
¼ –½	teaspoon herbal blend seasoning
⅛	teaspoon pepper
1	small potato, peeled and cubed
1	medium onion, cut into chunks
½	cup low-fat milk
1	bunch watercress (chopped small)

*See recipe.

1. In a heavy saucepan, combine all the above ingredients except the milk and simmer for about 20 minutes.

2. Take half of the soup mixture and place it in a blender, processing it until it is smooth. Repeat this with the other half of the soup mixture.

3. Return all the blended mixture to the saucepan along with milk. Cook over low heat, stirring constantly until heated through. Garnish with watercress.

Approximately 110 calories per bowl.

Athena's Cauliflower Quiche

1	8 – 10-ounce package of frozen cauliflower, cooked without salt and drained
½	cup cooked chopped broccoli
⅓ – ½	cup well-chopped onion
1	cup grated low-fat cheddar cheese
1	cup skim milk
3	eggs
⅓	cup whole-wheat pastry flour
½	teaspoon baking powder
	Dash of pepper
¼	teaspoon herbal blend seasoning
2	teaspoons oil

1. Chop the cooked cauliflower and place on paper towels (along with chopped broccoli) to complete the draining of moisture.

2. Lightly oil a nonstick pie plate with the two teaspoons of oil. Layer the cauliflower, broccoli, onion, and cheese in the pie plate.

3. Combine the remaining ingredients in a blender and process until smooth. Pour this mixture right over the vegetables in the pie plate.

4. Bake in a preheated 375-degree oven for about ½ hour or until the quiche has set well. Let it stand and cool for about 5 minutes before serving.

Makes 6 servings at approximately 180 calories each, or 4 larger servings at approximately 270 calories each.

Athena & Artemis' Bran Muffins

¼   cup safflower oil (or your favorite)
¼   cup blackstrap molasses
1   egg
⅔   cup skim milk
2   tablespoons honey
1   tablespoon baking powder
1   cup unprocessed bran
1   cup whole-wheat pastry flour
¼   teaspoon sea salt

Optional additions:

½   cup chopped nuts
½   cup chopped fruit (raisins, apples, dates, or mashed bananas)

1. Mix the first five ingredients together in a large mixing bowl.

2. Stir in the baking powder. Then add other dry ingredients and mix until dry ingredients are just moistened.

3. Fill lightly greased muffin cups two-thirds full. Bake in a pre-heated 400-degree oven for about 15 minutes.

Makes 1 dozen. Approximately 121 calories each, plain; 131 calories each with ¼ cup added raisins; 140 calories each with ¼ cup added chopped pecans; and 148 calories each with both ¼ cup raisins and ¼ cup pecans added.

Artemis' Glazed Carrots

    4   medium carrots
    ½   cup water for steaming (add more as needed)
    1   tablespoon honey (or to taste)

1. Peel and slice carrots and steam until tender, reserving 2 or more tablespoons of the liquid from steaming.

2. In a small pan, preferably nonstick, mix together the carrots, the reserved liquid, and the honey.

3. Heat through and serve.

Approximately 30 calories per serving.

Athena's Shish Kabob

    2   pounds lamb cut into 1½" cubes
         Cherry tomatoes
         Onion chunks
         Green pepper chunks
         Mushroom caps, fresh

Marinade:

Juice of 2 large lemons
3   tablespoons olive oil
2   tablespoons fresh grated onions with their juice
½   teaspoon black pepper
2   teaspoons crushed oregano (rubbed through hands)
¼   teaspoon salt (optional)
¼   teaspoon chili powder
3   cloves garlic, crushed

1. Stir together marinade and pour over the lamb. Marinate at least 2–4 hours or overnight. Stir once in a while.

2. Just before broiling, alternate the marinated lamb on skewers with cherry tomatoes, chunks of onion, chunks of green pepper, and mushroom caps.

3. Broil till done. You can serve a little of the marinade broth in a whole-grain pilaf-style dish for extra flavor.

Can serve four at approximately 300 calories per serving.

Artemis' Lentil-Rice Stew

¾   cup chopped onion
¾   cup chopped celery
1–2 teaspoons vegetable oil
6   cups water
¾   cup lentils (washed and sorted)
1   16-ounce can no-salt tomatoes, plus ½ can extra water if needed
¾   cup brown rice
1½ teaspoons garlic juice or garlic powder to taste

$\frac{1}{2}$ teaspoon basil (or more to taste)
$\frac{1}{2}$ teaspoon oregano (or more to taste)
$\frac{1}{4}$ teaspoon pepper
$\frac{1}{2}$ cup chopped zucchini

1. Sauté the onion and celery in the oil, in a medium-sized saucepan.

2. Add the water and the lentils and bring to a boil. Cover and simmer on low heat for 20 minutes.

3. Add everything else except the zucchini. Cover and simmer for 1 hour or until the rice is done.

4. Add the zucchini and cook 5 minutes more. Serve.

Makes 4–6 servings, approximately 155 calories per serving if made into 6 servings, or 230 calories per serving if made into 4 servings.

Athena's Baked Apples

2 apples, cored and the skin peeled off one ring around the top
$\frac{1}{2}$ cup fresh blueberries
$1\frac{1}{2}$ teaspoons honey

1. Fill the cored apples with $\frac{1}{4}$ cup each of the blueberries. Drizzle each apple with $\frac{3}{4}$ teaspoon of the honey.

2. Fill a deep baking pan with about $\frac{1}{4}$ inch water. Place apples in the water and bake in a preheated 350-degree oven for about $\frac{1}{2}$ hour, basting with their juices about every 10 minutes or so.

Serves 2 at approximately 110 calories per serving. To reduce to 80 calories a serving, substitute 1 teaspoon cinnamon for blueberries.

Artemis' Blueberry Jam Spread

    1   envelope unflavored gelatin
    ¾   cup water
    2   cups frozen blueberries (unsweetened)
    2   tablespoons honey
        Juice of ½ lemon

1. Combine gelatin and ¼ cup of the water and set aside.

2. Combine blueberries, remaining water, honey, and lemon juice. Simmer uncovered for 8 minutes.

3. Remove blueberries from heat and add gelatin mix and dissolve. Cool. Then pour into a glass jar. Cover tightly and refrigerate.

Contains 10 calories per tablespoon.

Balanced Nutrition Plan for
Apollo and Mercury

Selective Diet: High Protein, Low Fat

Apollo and Mercury require balanced diets high in protein and low in saturated fats. As long as they avoid fatty meats and fried foods, they can eat almost anything. They should limit their intake of alcohol and caffeine, since these drinks give them little nutrition and also hinder the thyroid's regulation of their metabolism. For the extra energy they need because of their thyroid vulnerability, it is important that they include animal protein such as lean red meat or fresh fish in their daily diets.

Priority Foods

- Red meat: lean cuts of beef, veal, and lamb only
- Fresh fish: all kinds
- Fowl: all kinds but those mentioned in "Limited" and "Avoidance Foods"
- Dairy: low-fat milk and cheese products only
- Vegetables: all kinds, especially green, at least three times a day; include legumes for protein

- Grains and cereals: bulgur and whole-wheat, rye, bran, oats, brown rice
- Fruits: fresh daily
- Nuts and seeds: almonds, pecans, walnuts, soy nuts, and sunflower and sesame seeds
- Oils: sunflower, sesame, safflower, and corn

Limited Foods

Pork, dark turkey meat, egg yolks, peanuts, peanut butter, avocados, bleached flour, refined sugars, and beverages containing alcohol and caffeine.

Avoidance Foods

Duck, processed meats, chicken and turkey skin, fried foods, whole milk and high-fat cheeses, ice cream, candies, commercial pastries, chocolate, nitrates, MSG (monosodium glutamate), and alcohol (except light beer and wine).

Vitamin and Mineral Requirements

100 mg. B-complex, 1000 mg. vitamin C, and one or two 4-in-1 combination capsules (with vitamin B-6, kelp, lecithin, and apple cider vinegar) daily. Extra minerals like calcium periodically.

Meal Timing

Three balanced meals, with occasional snacks. Avoid eating after 10:00 p.m., since your metabolism slows down then.

Morning meal	between 6:30 and 8:30 a.m.
Midmorning snack	between 10:30 and 11:30 a.m.
Midday meal	between noon and 2:00 p.m.
Midafternoon snack	between 2:30 and 3:30 p.m.
Evening meal	between 5:30 and 7:30 p.m.
Late snack	between 8:30 and 9:30 p.m.

Daily Instructions

- Drink at least six 8-ounce glasses of water daily.
- Never eat or drink as a substitute for emotional stress.
- Avoid midnight snacks whenever possible.
- Eat and drink slowly. Never eat when in a hurry.
- Enjoy experimenting with new health foods.

APOLLO & MERCURY WEIGHT-MANAGEMENT CHART

Height (Without Shoes)	Desired Weight (Pounds)			Calorie Allowance for Maintained Weight
	Small Frame	Medium Frame	Large Frame	
5' 4"	132 – 138	135 – 145	142 – 156	1500 – 1800
5"	134 – 140	137 – 148	144 – 160	1550 – 1850
6"	136 – 142	139 – 151	146 – 164	1600 – 1900
7"	138 – 145	142 – 154	149 – 168	1650 – 1950
8"	140 – 148	145 – 157	152 – 172	1700 – 2000
9"	142 – 151	148 – 160	155 – 176	1750 – 2050
10"	144 – 154	151 – 163	158 – 180	1800 – 2100
11"	146 – 157	154 – 166	161 – 184	1850 – 2150
6'0"	149 – 160	157 – 170	164 – 188	1900 – 2200
1"	152 – 164	160 – 174	168 – 192	1950 – 2250
2"	155 – 168	164 – 178	172 – 197	2000 – 2300
3"	158 – 172	167 – 182	176 – 202	2050 – 2350
4"	162 – 176	171 – 187	181 – 207	2100 – 2500

If you are an Apollo or Mercury and want to know if you are the proper weight for your height and weight, refer to the previous weight-management chart. This chart is based on standard insurance companies' data (Society of Actuaries and Association of Life Insurance Medical Directors of America, 1984).

The calorie allowances are for the ages twenty-five to fifty-nine. According to our statistics on Apollo men, most tend to be large framed, Mercury men tend to be medium framed. (The calorie allowances indicated here are based on data from the N.I.H. National Institute on Aging, Baltimore, Maryland.)

SEVEN-DAY MENU PLAN
APOLLO & MERCURY

DAY 1 • WEIGHT LOSS
(approximately 1100 calories)

Meal	Calories
BREAKFAST	
⅔ cup All-Bran cereal	140
½ cup skim milk	44
8 sliced strawberries	30
Cup of coffee	—
	214
LUNCH	
6 ounces broiled sirloin steak	350
1 cup cooked zucchini with pearl onions	30
1 slice 3-grain bread	78
1 pat butter (unsalted)	36
Perrier with lime slice	—
	494

DINNER

6 ounces broiled chicken leg and thigh (remove skin)	300
½ cup steamed broccoli	20
Salad of alfalfa sprouts, spinach, and scallions, with	20
2 tablespoons low-calorie Caesar dressing	22
Cup of hot herbal tea	—
	362

TOTAL CALORIES FOR THE DAY 1070

DAY 2 • WEIGHT LOSS
(approximately 1100 calories)

Meal	Calories

BREAKFAST

1 soft-boiled egg	80
1 bran muffin (made with no sugar) with	85
1 pat unsalted butter	36
½ cup hot apple cider	60
Cup of coffee	—
	261

LUNCH

4 ounces thinly sliced roast beef	408
1 cup cut asparagus, steamed	33
1 slice sprouted wheat bread	70
Cup of herbal tea	—
	511

SNACK

6 ounces low-sodium V-8 juice	35
1 Wasa crisp rye toast	39
	74

DINNER

6 ounces shellfish or 8 average shrimp (steamed, boiled, or baked)	200
Salad of cold artichoke heart, bibb lettuce, and green pepper rings, with	15
1 tablespoon apple cider vinegar and herbs	10
¼ small cantaloupe	30
Perrier with lemon slice	—
	255

TOTAL CALORIES FOR THE DAY   **1101**

DAY 3 • WEIGHT LOSS
(approximately 1100 calories)

Meal	Calories
BREAKFAST	
⅔ cup cooked oatmeal	101
½ cup skim milk	44
½ cup peaches (canned, in juice) or 1 fresh peach	35
Cup of coffee	—
	180

LUNCH

4 ounces broiled extra lean ground beef patty	140
1 whole-wheat pita bread	150
Broiled zucchini boats, sprinkled with paprika and dill weed	22
Watercress and spinach leaves salad with alfalfa sprouts, green pepper rings, and	30
1 tablespoon apple cider vinegar with 1 teaspoon sesame oil dressing	42
Iced herbal tea with lemon	—
	384

SNACK

½ cup cucumber slices and broccoli flowerets	20
3 Norwegian Flatbread crackers	60
Perrier with lime slice	—
	80

DINNER

6 ounces broiled swordfish steak	240
1 cup green beans, steamed	31
Salad of cooked artichoke hearts, chives, green onions, and watercress with	30
1 tablespoon low-calorie French dressing	20
½ cup fresh red raspberries with	37
½ cup plain skim milk yogurt	56
Cup of herbal tea	—
	414

TOTAL CALORIES FOR THE DAY   1058

DAY 4 • WEIGHT MAINTENANCE
(approximately 1600 calories)

Meal	Calories
BREAKFAST	
2 Shredded Wheat biscuits	180
¾ cup skim milk	66
½ cup cooked prunes	127
Cup of decaffeinated coffee	—
	373

SNACK	
6 ounces low-sodium V-8 juice	35
2 Rye Melba Rounds	40
	75

LUNCH	
1 serving Tuna Casserole*	255
Salad of 8 large romaine lettuce leaves,	
½ sliced tomato, ¼ cup sliced red onion,	
3 cooked artichoke hearts, and	
½ cup watercress, with	57
2 tablespoons low-calorie	
Thousand Island dressing	32
2 whole-wheat breadsticks	76
Glass of iced herbal tea	—
	420

SNACK	
Medium bunch of green seedless grapes	50
4 Triscuit crackers (low-sodium variety)	84
Perrier with lime slice	—
	134

*See recipe.

DINNER

6 ounces roasted light turkey meat (with skin removed)	300
1 cup steamed turnips with their greens	33
1 cup of green peas	100
1 serving Cranberry Salad* on bed of lettuce	95
Glass of white wine	90
	618

TOTAL CALORIES FOR THE DAY   1620

DAY 5 • WEIGHT MAINTENANCE
(approximately 1700 calories)

Meal	Calories

BREAKFAST

1 poached egg	82
1 slice rye toast	60
1 cup apple-cranberry juice	110
	252

LUNCH

6 ounces broiled chicken breast (remove skin)	231
Fresh spinach salad, tossed with 2 teaspoons sesame seeds; ½ medium orange, sectioned; and 3½ ounces tofu, cut up; topped with	168
2 tablespoons Honey-Poppyseed Dressing*	36
2 Wasa bread crisps	78
Glass of iced herbal tea	—
	513

*See recipe.

SNACK

1 glass low-fat milk	108
1 bran muffin	120
	228

DINNER

6 ounces broiled salmon fillet with dill and lemon slice	312
1 cup French-style green beans with	32
1 tablespoon chopped almonds	48
1 baked potato with 1 ounce sour cream and soy bacon bits	230
6 ounces low-sodium V-8 juice (on the rocks) with	35
1 large celery stick	7
1 wedge honeydew melon drizzled with lime juice	55
	719

TOTAL CALORIES FOR THE DAY   1712

DAY 6 • WEIGHT MAINTENANCE
(approximately 1800 calories)

Meal	Calories

BREAKFAST

½ cup Grape-Nuts cereal	200
1½ cups skim milk	44
½ cup whole strawberries	28
Cup of decaffeinated coffee	—
	272

SNACK

2 large stalks of celery with	16
2 tablespoons peanut butter	188
Cup of herbal tea	—
	204

LUNCH

1 bowl of Egg Drop Soup*	138
Stir-fry of 4 ounces scallops,	
2 teaspoons sesame oil, water chestnuts,	
scallions, Chinese black mushrooms,	
garlic, and ginger	275
¾ cup brown rice	174
Cup of hot Chinese tea	—
	587

SNACK

1 bran muffin	120
1 glass low-fat milk	145
	265

DINNER

2 lean lamb chops, broiled	250
1 baked potato with	103
1 pat unsalted butter	36
1 cup steamed brussels sprouts	56
1 Minty Fruit Cup*	80
Glass of iced mint tea	—
	525

TOTAL CALORIES FOR THE DAY   **1853**

*See recipe.

DAY 7 • FUN DAY
(approximately 2000 calories)

Meal	Calories
BREAKFAST	
1 whole-grain waffle, drizzled with	205
2 tablespoons maple syrup	100
6 ounces cranberry juice cocktail	144
Cup of coffee	—
	449
LUNCH	
1 Serving Cobb Salad* topped with	400
2 tablespoons whole-wheat croutons	44
½ cup orange sherbet topped with	129
1 tablespoon chopped pecans	52
Glass of iced herbal tea	—
	625
SNACK	
1 fresh Bartlett pear	100
1 ounce imported semisoft skim milk cheese	85
Perrier with lime slice	—
	185
DINNER	
Bowl of cold or hot Carrot Soup*	116
6 ounces lean sirloin strip steak, broiled	375
1 cup steamed broccoli flowerets	40
1 serving Brown Rice Salad*	30
2 glasses Burgundy wine	192
	753

TOTAL CALORIES FOR THE DAY   2012

*See recipe.

RECIPES FOR APOLLO & MERCURY'S MEAL PLANNING

Apollo's Egg Drop Soup

1½	tablespoons cornstarch
2	tablespoons water
4	cups chicken broth
1	tablespoon soy sauce (low-sodium variety)
4	eggs, lightly beaten
4	tablespoons chopped scallions

1. Blend the cornstarch and water together. Set aside.

2. In a saucepan, mix together the broth and soy sauce and bring to a boil.

3. One at a time, slowly pour eggs into the boiling broth, stirring gently as you add them.

4. Recombine cornstarch mixture, then add it to the soup. Continue cooking and stirring until the soup thickens.

5. Remove from heat, stir in scallions, and serve.

Makes 4 servings, approximately 138 calories per serving.

Mercury's Carrot Soup

1	pound carrots, washed and sliced with the ends cut off
3	cups chicken stock or natural canned broth (low sodium)
½	teaspoon thyme
¼	teaspoon pepper
1	medium onion, chopped

    1   clove garlic, minced
    1   teaspoon dill (dried or fresh)
    2   teaspoons safflower oil
    1½   cups plain low-fat yogurt

For garnish:
    Extra grated carrot and cucumber

1. Combine carrots, broth, thyme, and pepper and bring to a boil. Reduce to a simmer for about 10 minutes. Remove from heat and set aside.

2. In a separate small frying pan, sauté the onion and garlic with dill in the oil until tender. Set aside.

3. Divide the carrot and broth mixture in half and puree one-half at a time in the blender. Return to serving bowl and mix in the sautéed onion mixture. Add the yogurt and blend well.

4. Serve hot, or chill for several hours before serving, with grated carrot and cucumber garnish.

Serves 6, approximately 115 calories per serving.

Apollo's Cobb Salad

    24   ounces shrimp, shelled and deveined
    1   cup wax or yellow beans
    1   cup green beans
    1   cup precooked red kidney beans, drained
    2   cups chopped red cabbage
    2   cups diced potatoes
    1   cup green peas
    ½   cup low-calorie ranch dressing
         Mixed salad greens

1. Toss all ingredients together, with exception of salad greens. Chill.

2. To serve, arrange the salad greens on each salad plate or bowl. Center a scoop of above mixture on the greens. Top with whole-wheat croutons, if desired.

Serves 4, approximately 400 calories per serving.

Apollo's Cranberry Salad

1	16-ounce package fresh whole cranberries
2	cups water
½	cup honey
1	tablespoon unflavored gelatin
½	lemon, sliced
½	orange, sliced
	Parsley
	Lettuce

1. Boil cranberries over medium heat with water, honey, and gelatin until the cranberry skins pop.

2. Reduce heat to simmer an additional 10 minutes, until sauce begins to gel. Then remove from heat immediately and pour into mold or deep serving dish.

3. Arrange lemon and orange slices on top before mixture totally congeals. Top with chopped parsley and chill at least 2 hours.

4. Serve on a bed of lettuce. Excellent companion to fish or fowl.

Serves 8, approximately 92 calories per serving.

Mercury's Brown Rice Salad

1	10-ounce package frozen peas
½	cup brown rice
1	can water chestnuts (chopped)
½	teaspoon basil
¼	teaspoon tarragon
½	cup low-calorie Italian herb dressing
	Lettuce

1. Cook peas without salt, then drain and set aside.

2. Cook rice.

3. In a large bowl, add peas, rice, water chestnuts, and herbs. Pour dressing over all to coat lightly and delicately flavor. Blend gently.

4. Cover and chill in the bowl, a nice serving dish, or a mold.

5. To serve, spoon mixture onto lettuce leaves or shredded lettuce, or if a mold is used, turn the mold onto a bed of lettuce and serve.

Makes 4 servings, approximately 130 calories per serving.

Apollo & Mercury's Honey-Poppyseed Dressing

1	cup plain low-fat yogurt
1	tablespoon lemon juice
2	teaspoons poppy seeds
3	tablespoons honey
1	teaspoon dill (dried or fresh)

1. Mix all ingredients together well.

2. Chill 1 to 2 hours and serve.

Approximately 18 calories per tablespoon.

Mercury's Minty Fruit Cup

  ½   cup plain yogurt
  2   teaspoons lemon juice
2–3   teaspoons fresh chopped mint (or substitute ½–1 teaspoon dried)
  2   cups red or green seedless grapes, halved
  3   medium nectarines, cubed
  2   cups fresh pineapple, diced

1. Stir yogurt, lemon juice, and mint together. Set aside.

2. In serving bowl, combine all fruit and toss with yogurt mixture.

3. Chill and then serve.

Makes 8 servings, approximately 80 calories per serving.

Mercury's Tuna Casserole

  1   8-ounce bag spinach noodles
  2   teaspoons safflower or sesame oil
  1   cup peas with pearl onions, cooked without added salt
  1   6- or 7-ounce can water-packed tuna, drained
  ½   cup skim milk
  ¼   cup Parmesan cheese, grated
  ½   teaspoon paprika

1. Boil noodles with 1 teaspoon of oil added, until almost done. Drain and put noodles into a 1-quart casserole dish that has been lightly greased with the remaining 1 teaspoon of oil.

2. Add the peas and onions and tuna to the casserole. Pour the skim milk over all.

3. Sprinkle with the Parmesan cheese and paprika. Bake in a preheated 400-degree oven for 25 minutes.

Serves 4, approximately 225 calories per serving.

CHAPTER VII:

NUTRITION PLANS
ADRENAL VULNERABILITIES

Balanced Nutrition Plan
for Iris & Venus

Selective Diet: Low Sodium, Low Cholesterol

Iris and Venus fare best on low-sodium, low-cholesterol diets, since they are
vulnerable to hypertension and other circulatory diseases that can be trig-

gered or intensified by high levels of salt and cholesterol. For easy assimilation, they should eat foods that are high in mineral and fiber content, such as vegetables (both green and bulbar), fruits, and grains. They should limit their intake of most shellfish, dairy products, eggs, and fats and be especially careful with salt intake.

Priority Foods

- Animal proteins: chicken, fish, lean red meat (twice a week)
- Vegetables: all kinds
- Fruits: all kinds, including dried fruit
- Grains and cereals: all kinds, especially oats, bran, and wheat germ
- Legumes: soybeans, lentils, split peas, and chickpeas (good substitute for meat)
- Nuts and seeds: almonds, soy, pumpkin, and sunflower
- Oils: cold-pressed, all kinds
- Sprouts: alfalfa, mung beans, and bean sprouts
- Dairy: low-fat milk and skim milk cheeses

Limited Foods

Red meat, eggs, shrimp, crab, lobster, liver and other organ meats, citrus fruits, whole milk, butter, cheese (except low-fat), avocados, coconuts, cashews, peanuts, cocoa, and refined sugars. Limit alcohol intake to beer or wine, two glasses a day. Limit tea or coffee to two cups a day.

Avoidance Foods

Smoked and processed meats and fish, pork, fried food, table salt, soy sauce, pastry, chocolate, bleached flour, coconut oil, lard, MSG (monosodium glutamate), and foods with BHA, HBT, and TBHG preservatives.

Vitamin and Mineral Requirements

One high-potency B-C complex stress tab with zinc, 500 mg. vitamin B-5 (pantothenic acid), and 400 I.U. vitamin E daily. When under stress, take a mineral tab containing potassium, magnesium, and calcium daily.

Meal Timings

Three basic meals a day, with the heaviest at noon. Morning and evening snacks are permitted.

Morning meal . . . . .between 6:30 and 8:30 a.m.
Midmorning snack . . . . .between 10:30 and 11:30 a.m.
Midday meal . . . . .between noon and 2:00 p.m.
Evening meal . . . . .between 5:30 and 7:30 p.m.
Late snack .between 8:30 and 9:30 p.m.

Daily Instructions

- Drink at least four 8-ounce glasses of water or herbal tea daily.

- Whenever possible, rest after your main meal, elevating your feet for about fifteen minutes.

- Eat red meat only at the noon meal.

- Create a relaxed environment for at least one meal a day.

- Enjoy a daily relaxing tonic, such as a glass of white wine or beer with the evening meal.

IRIS & VENUS
WEIGHT-MANAGEMENT CHART

Height (Without Shoes)	Desired Weight (Pounds)			Calorie Allowance for Maintained Weight
	Small Frame	Medium Frame	Large Frame	
4' 10"	102 – 111	109 – 121	118 – 131	900 – 1000
11"	103 – 113	111 – 123	120 – 134	950 – 1100
5' 0"	104 – 115	113 – 126	122 – 137	1000 – 1200
1"	106 – 118	115 – 129	125 – 140	1050 – 1250
2"	108 – 121	118 – 132	128 – 143	1100 – 1300
3"	111 – 124	121 – 135	131 – 147	1150 – 1350
4"	114 – 127	124 – 138	134 – 151	1200 – 1400
5"	117 – 130	127 – 141	137 – 155	1250 – 1450
6"	120 – 133	130 – 144	140 – 159	1300 – 1500
7"	123 – 137	133 – 147	143 – 163	1350 – 1550
8"	126 – 139	136 – 150	146 – 167	1400 – 1600
9"	129 – 142	139 – 153	149 – 170	1450 – 1650
10"	132 – 145	142 – 156	152 – 173	1500 – 1700
11"	135 – 148	145 – 159	155 – 176	1550 – 1750
6' 0"	138 – 151	148 – 162	158 – 179	1600 – 1800

If you are an Iris or Venus and want to know if you are the proper weight for your height and structure, refer to the above weight-management chart. This chart is based on standard insurance companies' data (Society of Actuaries and Association of Life Insurance Medical Directors of America, 1984).

The calorie allowances are for ages twenty-five to fifty-nine. These ages represent most women in the United States today. According to our statistics on these women, most tend to be of medium bone structure.

For those under twenty-five or over fifty-nine, the calorie allowances vary slightly from individual to individual, though in general, more calories are needed in youth and fewer in the senior years, due to differences in life-style activities. (The calorie allowances indicated here are based on data from the N.I.H. National Institute on Aging, Baltimore, Maryland.)

SEVEN-DAY MENU PLAN
IRIS & VENUS

DAY 1 • WEIGHT LOSS
(approximately 1000 calories)

Meal	Calories
BREAKFAST	
1 soft-boiled egg	80
1 bran muffin or 1 whole-wheat biscuit	121
½ cup fresh grapefruit sections	39
Cup of coffee	—
	240
SNACK	
6 ounces low-sodium V-8 juice	25
2 Norwegian Flatbreads	40
	65
LUNCH	
Open-face sandwich made with	
3 ounces sliced roast turkey (white meat)	240
On 1 slice sprouted-wheat bread	75
Mixed green salad of watercress, alfalfa	
sprouts, and cucumber slices, with	20

1 tablespoon wine vinegar and sesame oil dressing	42
Iced herbal tea with lemon peel	—
	377

DINNER

4 ounces baked salmon steak with lemon slice	160
1 cup steamed broccoli flowerets	40
½ small baked acorn squash with cinnamon	86
Salad of shredded cabbage with carrots, with sesame seeds and apple cider vinegar	40
Small bunch of green seedless grapes	35
Cup of Postum	—
	361

TOTAL CALORIES FOR THE DAY   1043

DAY 2 • WEIGHT LOSS
(approximately 1000 calories)

Meal	Calories

BREAKFAST

1 cup Wheatena	160
½ cup skim milk	44
½ cup sliced strawberries	28
Cup of decaffeinated or regular coffee	—
	232

SNACK

1 No-Flour Corn Muffin*	62
Cup of hot herbal tea	—
	62

*See recipe.

LUNCH

1 serving Stir-Fried Garlic Ginger Chicken*	250
1/2 cup of brown rice	116
1 8-ounce Natural Fruit Gelatin*	50
Perrier with lemon	—
	416

DINNER

4 ounces shellfish (except shrimp), steamed boiled, or baked	100
Salad of cold artichoke hearts, bibb lettuce, and green pepper rings, with apple cider vinegar and	30
1 teaspoon safflower oil	42
1 slice of 7-grain bread	82
¼ small cantaloupe	30
Cup of hot water with lemon	—
	284

TOTAL CALORIES FOR THE DAY   994

DAY 3 • WEIGHT LOSS
(approximately 1000 calories)

Meal	Calories

BREAKFAST

⅔ cup oatmeal	88
½ cup skim milk	45
1 fresh peach, sliced	40
Cup of coffee	—
	173

*See recipe.

SNACK

1 slice 7-grain bread	75
½ ounce skim milk cheese	35
Cup of Pero or herbal tea	—
	110

LUNCH

3 ounces lean loin lamb chop	300
½ cup boiled parslied potatoes with skins	60
½ cup steamed green beans	15
Hot herbal tea	—
	375

DINNER

4 ounces broiled flounder fillet	135
1 cup steamed zucchini with pearl onions	32
Salad of sliced beets, green pepper rings, red and green leaf lettuce, and sprouts, with	32
2 tablespoons Honey Yogurt-Caraway Seed Dressing*	40
Cup of decaffeinated coffee	—
	239

SNACK

½ cup low-sodium V-8 juice	25
4 Wheat Thins	40
	65

TOTAL CALORIES FOR THE DAY   962

*See recipe.

DAY 4 • WEIGHT MAINTENANCE
(approximately 1200 calories)

Meal	Calories

BREAKFAST

1 cup puffed rice	60
½ cup skim milk	44
½ cup fresh sliced strawberries	28
Cup of coffee	—
	132

SNACK

½ pink grapefruit with	53
2 teaspoons honey	43
Cup of herbal tea	—
	96

LUNCH

3 ounces lean roast beef (sliced)	224
1 small baked potato with chives	125
½ cup peas and carrots	45
1 medium baked apple	110
8-ounce glass of iced tea with lemon	—
	504

DINNER

Bowl of Vegetable Barley Soup*	120
2 whole-wheat breadsticks	72
Salad with artichoke hearts, red sweet peppers, cold asparagus, and capers on a bed of escarole, with	80

*See recipe.

½ tablespoon oil and apple cider vinegar	70
1 light beer (8 ounces)	100
	442

TOTAL CALORIES FOR THE DAY   1174

DAY 5 • WEIGHT MAINTENANCE
(approximately 1200 calories)

Meal	Calories

BREAKFAST

1 cup of Honey Bran Flakes	132
½ cup of skim milk	44
1 sliced banana	127
Cup of coffee	—
	303

SNACK

4 ounces cranberry juice cocktail	80
10 roasted unsalted almonds	60
	140

LUNCH

4 ounces broiled bluefish with herb seasoning and ½ pat unsalted butter	180
Spinach salad with sliced mushrooms and soy bacon bits, with	40
1 tablespoon vinaigrette and garlic dressing	30
½ broiled tomato with Parmesan cheese	35
Cup of herbal tea	—
1 serving of Strawberry Mousse*	110
	395

*See recipe.

DINNER

1 serving of Tarragon Chicken in Wine*	177
½ cup of steamed broccoli	25
1 No-Flour Corn Muffin* with corn oil margarine	100
8-ounce white wine and Perrier cocktail	50
	352

TOTAL CALORIES FOR THE DAY 1190

DAY 6 • WEIGHT MAINTENANCE
(approximately 1200 calories)

Meal	Calories

BREAKFAST

1 slice French toast made with sprouted-wheat bread	120
1 tablespoon maple syrup	50
½ small canteloupe	58
Cup of coffee	—
	228

SNACK

1 cup sliced mixed vegetables with	40
2 tablespoons low-fat Cucumber-Yogurt Dip*	20
Iced herbal tea	—
	60

LUNCH

4 ounces broiled lean veal steak basted with	245
Low-calorie Italian dressing	20
1 boiled potato in skin	104

*See recipe.

½ cup diced beets	32
Salad of mixed green leaves with	22
1 tablespoon oil and vinegar dressing	42
Cup of decaffeinated coffee	—
	465

DINNER

1 cup split pea soup	213
Pasta salad made with ½ cup cooked noodles	100
1 chopped green onion, 1 tomato, and	
1 cucumber on bed of bibb lettuce and	30
1 tablespoon safflower mayonnaise	60
1 fresh plum	32
Perrier and lime peel	—
	435

TOTAL CALORIES FOR THE DAY   1188

DAY 7 • FUN DAY
(approximately 1500 calories)

Meal	Calories

BREAKFAST

2 buckwheat pancakes with	108
1 pat unsalted butter	33
2 tablespoons honey or syrup	100
1 slice fresh pineapple	39
Cup of coffee or tea	—
	280

SNACK

10 unsalted roasted almonds	62
Cup of herbal tea	—
	62

LUNCH

½ Cornish hen (baked or broiled)	200
½ cup steamed brown or wild rice	110
¾ cup baby brussels sprouts	35
½ cup fresh red raspberries with	40
6 ounces plain low-fat yogurt	92
Perrier and lime	—
	477

DINNER

4 ounces Alaskan king crabmeat	160
Stir fried with 2 teaspoons light soy sauce	
and 2 teaspoons sesame oil and	94
½ cake bean curd (tofu),	43
4 ounces Chinese mushrooms,	19
4 ounces water chestnuts, and	90
4 ounces Chinese snow peas	36
4-ounce glass of white wine	90
½ cup canned mandarin orange slices	45
	577

SNACK

1 large fig bar or slice of	
Cranberry Wheatgerm Bread*	101
Cup of herbal tea	—
	101

TOTAL CALORIES FOR THE DAY   **1497**

*See recipe.

RECIPES FOR IRIS & VENUS' MEAL PLANNING

Iris' Vegetable Barley Soup

2	pounds beef soup bone (shin bone is the best)
2	tablespoons safflower oil
2	large onions, chopped in large pieces
1	tablespoon of pot herbs (thyme/sage/bay leaf/parsley)
½	cup barley
1	rutabaga, peeled and cubed
1	small bunch of carrots, sliced
3	medium potatoes, cubed with skins on
½	small head cabbage, cut up
4	pieces of celery stalk, cut into ½-inch pieces
2	cups of no-salt canned tomatoes, chopped up
2	cups of chopped broccoli, flowers and stems together

1. Place soup bone, safflower oil, onions, and herbs in 6-quart cooking pot and fill with cold water to 3 inches from top. Bring to boil and simmer for 1 hour.

2. Cool and skim the grease off the top. Then add remaining ingredients. Cook on medium heat for another 30 minutes and serve.

Delicious, and only 120 calories per large bowl serving.

Iris' Honey Yogurt-Caraway Seed Dressing

1	8-ounce container of plain low-fat yogurt
3	tablespoons honey

4 teaspoons lemon juice

2 teaspoons caraway seeds (whole)

Blend all ingredients together and serve.
Good on fruit salads.

Approximately 20 calories per tablespoon.

Iris & Venus' Cucumber-Yogurt Dip or Dressing

1 cup plain low-fat yogurt

1 medium cucumber, peeled and chopped

1 teaspoon soy bacon bits

1 tablespoon prepared horseradish

Place all ingredients in a blender and process until smooth.

Approximately 10 calories per tablespoon.

Iris & Venus' Cranberry Wheat Germ Bread

2 cups sifted whole-wheat flour

2 teaspoons low-sodium baking powder

2 teaspoons low-sodium baking soda

1 cup raw cranberries, halved

½ cup chopped nuts (pecans or walnuts preferred)

½ cup wheat germ

3 tablespoons grated orange peel

½ cup orange juice

1 egg, slightly beaten

¾ cup honey

½ cup warm water

2 tablespoons salad oil

1. Mix and sift flour, baking powder, and baking soda. Stir in cranberry halves, nuts, wheat germ, and orange peel.

2. In another bowl combine egg, orange juice, water, honey, and oil. Add this to flour mixture.

3. Stir until just moistened. Spoon into greased loaf pan and bake at 350 degrees for 50–60 minutes or until a knife inserted in the middle comes out clean. Cool in pan for 5 minutes, then finish cooling on cake rack.

Approximately 100 calories per small slice.

Venus' No-Flour Corn Muffins

1	cup of cornmeal
½	teaspoon low-sodium baking soda
½	teaspoon low-sodium baking powder
1	cup minus 2 tablespoons skim milk to which
2–3	tablespoons lemon juice is added
½	cup cooked corn
1	egg, beaten
1	tablespoon low-calorie margarine
	Vegetable oil spray coating for muffin tins

1. Combine all dry ingredients and mix them well.

2. Add milk-lemon juice mixture, corn, egg, and margarine and mix until well blended.

3. Coat muffin tin lightly with the oil spray. Spoon batter into cups about ⅔ full. Bake in a preheated 450-degree oven for about 10–12 minutes.

Makes 12 muffins at about 62 calories each.

Iris' Tarragon Chicken in Wine

    8   pieces chicken breast with skins removed
    1   pound fresh mushrooms, sliced in thick pieces
    1   cup whole-wheat pasta shells
    1   cup white wine, plus 1 cup water
    1   tablespoon dried parsley
    2   teaspoons dried tarragon
    $\frac{1}{2}$ teaspoon fresh ground pepper

1. In a rectangular glass baking dish, arrange chicken with the bone side down.

2. Scatter mushrooms and pasta around the chicken. Pour the wine and water over the top, then sprinkle with the herbs and seasonings.

3. Cover and bake in a 350-degree oven for about an hour or until the chicken is tender.

Serves 8, about 177 calories per serving.

Venus' Stir-Fried Garlic Ginger Chicken

   16   ounces deboned chicken breasts, cut into bite-sized pieces
    1   tablespoon low-sodium soy sauce
    1   tablespoon white wine
    $\frac{1}{2}$ teaspoon cornstarch or arrowroot
    1   tablespoon sesame or other oil
    2   tablespoons chopped fresh ginger root or ground ginger to taste
    1   tablespoon chopped fresh garlic or garlic powder to taste

ᑲ

> 2   cups fresh snow peas
> 1–2   cups Chinese celery cabbage, fresh broccoli, or green
>   cabbage, chopped
> 1   cup sliced water chestnuts
> ½–1   whole cake of tofu (soybean curd), cut into small pieces
> ½   cup chopped green onion, including tops

1. Combine chicken, soy sauce, wine, and cornstarch or arrowroot and let stand for 15 minutes.

2. In large frying pan or wok, heat oil, ginger, and garlic. Add the
   chicken mixture and stir-fry until chicken changes color.

3. Add remaining ingredients and stir-fry for an additional 3–5
   minutes. Season further, if desired, and serve.

Makes 4 servings, approximately 250 calories each.

Iris & Venus' Natural Fruit Gelatin

> 1   package unflavored gelatin (such as Knox)
> 2   cups of apple-cranberry juice (unsweetened)
> 1   tablespoon honey
> 1   can water- or juice-packed fruit cocktail, if desired

1. Bring the juice to a boil, stir in honey, and remove from stove.

2. Sprinkle in gelatin and stir until dissolved.

3. Pour into desired serving dish and add fruit cocktail.
   Refrigerate for several hours or overnight.

Variations:

Use orange-pineapple juice with a bit of shredded coconut and sliced bananas, or lime juice with diet ginger ale and mandarin orange slices, or apple juice or cider and pears, or low sodium V-8 juice with shredded cheddar cheese.

Makes about 8 servings, approximately 50 calories each.

Venus' Strawberry Mousse

  1   envelope unflavored gelatin
 ½   cup water
 ⅔   cup instant nonfat dry milk powder
  2   tablespoons honey (or less if preferred)
 ¾   cup frozen unsweetened strawberries (thawed)
 ½   teaspoon vanilla extract
  6   ice cubes

1. Put water in a saucepan and sprinkle gelatin over. Let stand for 1 minute, then cook on medium heat, stirring constantly, for another minute or until gelatin is dissolved.

2. Combine gelatin and remaining ingredients except ice cubes in a blender and process until well blended.

3. Add ice cubes 1 or 2 at a time and process until smooth.

4. Pour into 4 dessert dishes. Cover and refrigerate about 2 hours or overnight.

Approximately 110 calories per serving.

Balanced Nutrition Plan for Neptune & Bacchus

Selective Diet: Low Sodium, Low Cholesterol

Neptune and Bacchus fare best on low-sodium, low-cholesterol diets, since they are vulnerable to hypertension and other circulatory diseases that can be triggered or intensified by high levels of salt and cholesterol. For easy assimilation, they should try to eat foods that are high in mineral and fiber content, such as vegetables (both green and bulbar), fruits, and grains. They should also limit their intake of most shellfish, dairy products, eggs, nuts, and especially salt.

Priority Foods

- Animal proteins: chicken, fish, lean red meat (twice a week)
- Vegetables: all kinds
- Fruits: all kinds, including dried fruit
- Grains and cereals: all kinds, especially oats, bran, and wheat germ
- Legumes: soybeans, lentils, split peas, mung beans, navy beans, kidney beans, and black beans (good substitute for meat)

- Nuts and seeds: almonds, walnuts, soy nuts, pumpkin seeds, and sunflower seeds
- Oils: cold-pressed (all kinds)
- Sprouts: alfalfa, wheat, and bean sprouts
- Dairy: low-fat milk and skim milk cheeses

Limited Foods

Red meat, eggs, shrimp, crab, lobster, liver and other organ meats, citrus fruits, whole milk, butter, cheese (except low-fat), avocados, coconuts, cashews, peanuts, cocoa, and refined sugars. Limit alcohol to two glasses a day of beer or wine. Limit tea or coffee to two cups a day. Limit citrus with meals.

Avoidance Foods

Smoked and processed meats and fish, pork, fried foods, table salt, soy sauce, pastry, chocolate, bleached flour, coconut oil, lard, MSG (monosodium glutamate), and foods containing BHA, BHT, and TBHG preservatives.

Vitamin and Mineral Requirements

One high-potency B-C complex stress tab with zinc, 500 mg. vitamin B-5 (pantothenic acid), and 400 I.U. vitamin E daily. When under stress, take a mineral tab containing potassium, magnesium, and calcium each day.

Meal Timing

Three basic meals a day, with the heaviest at noon. Morning and evening snacks are permitted.

Morning meal . . . . .between 6:30 and 8:30 a.m.
Midmorning snack . . . . .between 10:30 and 11:30 a.m.

Midday meal ....between noon and 2:00 p.m.
Evening meal ....between 5:30 and 7:30 p.m.
Late snack ....between 8:30 and 9:30 p.m.

Daily Instructions

- Drink at least four 8-ounce glasses of water daily.

- Whenever possible, rest after your noon meal, elevating your feet for about fifteen minutes.

- Eat red meat only at the noon meal.

- Choose a serene environment for at least one meal a day.

- In the evening, enjoy a daily relaxing tonic such as a glass of white wine or beer.

NEPTUNE & BACCHUS
WEIGHT-MANAGEMENT CHART

Height (Without Shoes)	Desired Weight (Pounds) Small Frame	Medium Frame	Large Frame	Calorie Allowance for Maintained Weight
5' 4"	132 – 138	135 – 145	142 – 156	1500 – 1800
5"	134 – 140	137 – 148	144 – 160	1550 – 1850
6"	136 – 142	139 – 151	146 – 164	1600 – 1900
7"	138 – 145	142 – 154	149 – 168	1650 – 1950
8"	140 – 148	145 – 157	152 – 172	1700 – 2000
9"	142 – 151	148 – 160	155 – 176	1750 – 2050
10"	144 – 154	151 – 163	158 – 180	1800 – 2100
11"	146 – 157	154 – 166	161 – 184	1850 – 2150

6' 0"	149 – 160	157 – 170	164 – 188	1900 – 2200
1"	152 – 164	160 – 174	168 – 192	1950 – 2250
2"	155 – 168	164 – 178	172 – 197	2000 – 2300
3"	158 – 172	167 – 182	176 – 202	2050 – 2350
4"	162 – 176	171 – 187	181 – 207	2100 – 2500

If you are a Neptune or Bacchus and want to know if you are the proper weight for your height and structure, refer to the above weight-management chart. This chart is based on standard insurance companies' data (Society of Actuaries and Association of Life Insurance Medical Directors of America, 1984).

The calorie allowances are for ages twenty-five to fifty-nine. According to our statistics on Neptune and Bacchus men, most tend to be of medium frame. (The calorie allowances indicated here are based on data from the N.I.H. National Institute on Aging, Baltimore, Maryland.)

SEVEN-DAY MENU PLAN
NEPTUNE & BACCHUS

DAY 1 • WEIGHT LOSS
(approximately 1100 calories)

Meal	Calories
BREAKFAST	
1 soft-boiled egg	80
1 whole-wheat biscuit	85
½ cup cranberry juice cocktail	60
Cup of coffee	—
	225

SNACK

6 slices raw cucumber	4
3 raw celery stalks	9
2 tablespoons Dilled Yogurt Dressing*	16
Cup of decaffeinated coffee or herbal tea	—
	29

LUNCH

6 ounces broiled swordfish with lemon	220
2 small parslied potatoes	80
1 cup steamed broccoli flowerets	40
Salad of green and red leaf lettuce with chopped pimentos and chives	40
1 tablespoon Vinaigrette Dressing*	20
1 large slice of canteloupe	40
Cup of Postum or hot herbal tea with ½ teaspoon honey	10
	450

DINNER

Chef's salad consisting of 4 ounces cubed white turkey meat on a bed of	160
Mixed salad greens of spinach leaves, bibb lettuce, topped with alfalfa sprouts, and	16
1 tablespoon unsalted sunflower seeds	42
2 tablespoons low-calorie ranch dressing	30
2 sesame seed breadsticks	84
1 medium red apple	60
Herbal iced tea	—
	392

TOTAL CALORIES FOR THE DAY   1096

*See recipe.

DAY 2 • WEIGHT LOSS
(approximately 1100 calories)

Meal	Calories
BREAKFAST	
1 cup oatmeal	132
½ cup skim milk	44
Stewed fruit compote of 2 apricot halves and 2 prunes	80
Cup of coffee	—
	256
SNACK	
1 bran muffin	120
1 pat unsalted butter	36
Cup of hot water with lemon wedge	2
	158
LUNCH	
1 cup cold Gazpacho*	40
4 ounces broiled chicken breast with skin removed	150
Broiled zucchini boat, sprinkled with paprika and dill weed	22
Salad of watercress, spinach leaves, alfalfa sprouts, and green pepper rings, with	10
1 tablespoon low-calorie herb and garlic dressing	30
Iced herbal tea with lemon wedge	2
	254

*See recipe.

DINNER

6 large oysters (steamed, raw, or baked)	150
Tossed salad of cold artichoke hearts, sliced tomatoes, bibb lettuce, and green pepper rings	35
2 tablespoons Vinaigrette Dressing*	40
1 slice whole-grain garlic toast	100
10 whole strawberries, topped with	37
⅓ cup plain yogurt	40
Perrier with lime slice	—
	402

TOTAL CALORIES FOR THE DAY   1070

DAY 3 • WEIGHT LOSS
(approximately 1100 calories)

Meal	Calories

BREAKFAST

1 cup bran flakes	104
1 cup skim milk	88
1 medium banana	120
Cup of hot tea or coffee	—
	312

SNACK

1 slice 7-grain bread	80
1 ounce low-fat cream cheese spread	55
Cup of hot herbal tea	—
	135

*See recipe.

LUNCH

6 ounces broiled flounder with herb seasonings	120
1 boiled red potato in skin	105
1 cup steamed green beans	32
Small bunch of seedless white grapes	50
Cup of decaffeinated coffee	—
	307

MIDAFTERNOON SNACK

Perrier with lime	—

DINNER

1 serving of Hawaiian Chicken Dinner*	300
1 serving of Tomato Aspic Salad* on bed of greens with watercress garnish	35
Iced herbal tea	—
	335

TOTAL CALORIES FOR THE DAY   **1089**

DAY 4 • WEIGHT MAINTENANCE
(approximately 1500 calories)

Meal	Calories

BREAKFAST

½ pink grapefruit†	80
1 poached egg on	80
1 slice whole-wheat toast	75
Cup of coffee	—
	235

†Citrus eaten prior to (not after) dairy products will normally not cause digestive difficulty.

*See recipe.

SNACK

6 ounces low-sodium V-8 juice	35
1 unsalted rice cake	36
Cup of hot herbal tea	—
	71

LUNCH

2 ounces broiled loin lamb chop	185
½ cup of steamed yellow squash with diced onion	20
Spinach salad with mushroom slices and soy bacon bits	40
1 tablespoon vinaigrette with honey dressing	30
1 whole-wheat roll	90
1 pat unsalted butter	36
1 plum (fresh)	29
1 4-ounce glass of rosé wine	120
	550

DINNER

6 ounces salmon steak, baked or broiled	270
1 baked potato (large)	140
1 ounce sour cream with chives	57
10 asparagus spears, steamed	30
Perrier with lime slice	—
½ cup fruit sherbet	130
	627

LATE SNACK

1 8-ounce glass skim milk	88
2 Rye Melba Rounds	40
	128

TOTAL CALORIES FOR THE DAY   **1611**

DAY 5 • WEIGHT MAINTENANCE
(*approximately 1600 calories*)

Meal	Calories

BREAKFAST

1 cup cooked bulgur, topped with cinnamon, 1 teaspoon honey, and	300
4 slivered almonds	78
½ large peach (canned in juice)	33
Cup of coffee	—
	411

SNACK

1 Whole-Wheat Blueberry Muffin*	120
Cup of herbal tea with lemon	2
	122

LUNCH

1 4-ounce serving of beef pot roast with	219
Fresh parsley sprinkling	4
½ cup mashed potatoes (made with skim milk)	126
½ cup boiled sliced carrots	24
½ cup coleslaw (made with safflower oil mayonnaise)	85
1 4-ounce glass Burgundy wine	96
½ cup melon balls	52
	606

DINNER

1 bowl of vegetarian vegetable soup	150
1 slice pumpernickel bread	79

*See recipe.

1 pat unsalted butter	36
Tossed salad of artichoke hearts, radish slices, green pepper rings, cucumber slices, celery slices, fresh dill, and watercress with romaine lettuce leaves	62
2 tablespoons Vinaigrette Dressing*	40
Perrier with lime slice	—
	367

SNACK

10 strawberries, sliced	37
½ cup plain low-fat yogurt	60
Cup of hot herbal tea	—
	97

TOTAL CALORIES FOR THE DAY   1603

DAY 6 • WEIGHT MAINTENANCE
(*approximately 1700 calories*)

Meal	Calories

BREAKFAST

1 cup cooked rolled oats	132
½ cup skim milk	44
1 cup hot apple cider with cinnamon	118
	294

SNACK

6 sliced celery and carrot sticks	36
3 tablespoons Dilled Yogurt Dressing*	30
Cup of coffee, regular or decaffeinated	—
	66

*See recipe.

LUNCH

1 large serving (2 cups) plain Linguini (made with whole-wheat or soy flour)	360
1 serving White Clam Sauce*	95
Caesar salad with romaine lettuce, egg, garlic, mustard, and anchovies	150
2 tablespoons whole-wheat bread crumbs	44
1 4-ounce glass of white wine	90
	739

DINNER

4 ounces broiled, sliced veal tenderloin	245
1 serving baked Ratatouille Niçoise*	144
4 ounces canned (in juice) pear salad, with	53
Low-fat cottage cheese filling on	42
Bibb lettuce	4
Iced or hot herbal tea with lemon	2
	490

LATE SNACK

2 cups plain popcorn, popped in 2 teaspoons safflower oil	120
1 diet soda drink (no caffeine)	3
	123

TOTAL CALORIES FOR THE DAY 1712

*See recipe.

DAY 7 • FUN DAY
(approximately 1700 calories)

Meal	Calories

BREAKFAST

6 ounces cranberry juice cocktail	90
2 buckwheat pancakes	108
2 pats corn oil margarine	72
2 tablespoons maple syrup	100
Cup of coffee	—
	370

LUNCH

1 cup Pumpkin Soup*	78
1 whole (small) baked Cornish hen	250
1/2 cup wild rice cooked with herbs	180
2/3 cup steamed broccoli	26
1 baked apple with cinnamon and honey	85
Perrier with lime	—
	619

DINNER

6 ounces lean beef fillet	300
1 small baked potato, with	120
2 tablespoons sour cream and chives	57
Salad of lettuce, sliced tomatoes, cucumber, and red onion	38
2 tablespoons low-calorie Italian dressing	16
1 4-ounce glass of red Bordeaux wine	96
3/4 cup of raw red raspberries	57

*See recipe.

1 ounce half-and-half cream	40
Cup of decaffeinated coffee	—
	724

TOTAL CALORIES FOR THE DAY   **1713**

RECIPES FOR NEPTUNE & BACCHUS' MEAL PLANNING

Neptune & Bacchus' Gazpacho

1	16-ounce can no-salt tomatoes
2	small cans low-sodium V-8 juice
1	cucumber, peeled and diced
1–2	stalks celery, diced
1	medium green pepper, chopped
1	small onion, diced
1	teaspoon apple cider vinegar
2	cloves garlic, crushed
	Pepper and other seasonings to taste

1. Throw all into blender and process until smooth.

2. Chill for several hours. Top with additional chopped vegetables and/or croutons if desired.

Makes 4 servings, about 80 calories each, or 6 servings, about 52 calories each.

ॐ

Neptune's Pumpkin Soup

　1　tablespoon safflower oil
　½　cup finely chopped onions
　3　cups plain canned pumpkin
　1½　cups chicken stock
　1½　cups skim milk
　　　Pumpkin pie spice
　　　Nutmeg

1. Sauté onions in oil in a heavy pot until soft.

2. Stir in pumpkin and chicken stock alternately, blend until smooth.

3. Add spice to taste.

4. Bring to a boil and then simmer on low heat for 10 minutes, stirring constantly so as not to burn.

5. Sprinkle with nutmeg and serve.

Makes 6 cups, approximately 78 calories per serving.

Bacchus' Tomato Aspic Salad

　2　cups low-sodium V-8 juice
　2　cups no-salt canned tomatoes, pureed
　1　teaspoon dried herbs
　　　(parsley/celery flakes/pepper/bay leaf)
　1½　packages unflavored gelatin (4 teaspoons)
　1　teaspoon honey
　1　tablespoon lemon juice
　½　teaspoon Worcestershire sauce

$\frac{1}{4}$ teaspoon salt substitute
     Salad greens
     Watercress

1. Pour 1$\frac{1}{2}$ cups V-8 juice and pureed tomatoes in saucepan.
   Add herbs and bring to a boil.

2. Mix gelatin and remaining $\frac{1}{2}$ cup juice together. Stir in honey,
   lemon, Worcestershire sauce, and salt substitute.

3. Add gelatin mixture to the hot juice mixture and stir until well
   blended. Then cool for 10 minutes and pour into aspic mold.

4. Chill until firm. Invert mold on salad greens and garnish with
   watercress.

Serves 8 at approximately 45 calories per serving.

Bacchus' Vinaigrett Dressing

     3   tablespoons sesame or safflower oil
     1   cup apple cider vinegar
     3   tablespoons water
   1–2   cloves garlic (crushed through a garlic press)
     1   teaspoon dry mustard
   $\frac{1}{2}$ teaspoon mixed dried herbs
          (oregano, basil, and parsley)

1. Combine all ingredients.

2. Blend and chill until ready to serve. Shake well before serving.

Makes about 1$\frac{1}{4}$ cups, approximately 20 calories per tablespoon.

Neptune's Dilled Yogurt Dressing

½   cup plain low-fat yogurt
½   cup skim milk
1   tablespoon lemon juice
1   tablespoon minced onion
½   cucumber, peeled and minced
¾   teaspoon dill
½   teaspoon garlic powder
    Dash of pepper

1. Combine all ingredients in a mixing bowl and with a whisk blend until smooth.

2. Chill about 2 hours, then serve.

Approximately 10 calories per serving.

Neptune's Whole-Wheat Blueberry Muffins

3   cups whole-wheat flour
1   teaspoon baking powder
1   teaspoon salt substitute
½   cup dry nonfat milk powder
¾   stick corn oil margarine
1   tablespoon honey
2   tablespoons blackstrap molasses
2   slightly beaten egg whites
1   cup water
1   cup fresh blueberries (soaked in water for 20 minutes, then drained)

1. Sift together dry ingredients, set aside.

2. In mixing bowl, blend margarine, honey, molasses, and beaten egg whites.

3. Add dry mixture, blending all together with water until smooth.

4. Fold in blueberries, being careful not to damage them, and fill large muffin cups half full.

5. Bake at 375 degrees for 35 minutes or until tops split.

Approximately 120 calories per large muffin, 90 calories per small.

Neptune's Linguini and White Clam Sauce

    1   garlic clove, minced
    1   small onion, finely chopped
    1   tablespoon safflower oil
    2   cups chicken stock*
    1   tablespoon Italian herbs, or more to taste
    1   can minced clams in liquid

*You can make your own chicken stock by boiling chicken backs in water with celery and onion to taste. It should be cooled and skimmed for low cholesterol.

1. Sauté onion and garlic in oil until golden but not brown.

2. Add chicken stock and herbs.

3. Bring to a boil while slowly adding clams. Do not overcook, as clams will toughen.

4. Serve over cooked whole-grain linguini. (Either whole-wheat, soy, or artichoke pasta is an excellent substitute for white-flour pasta.)

Serves 4, approximately 95 calories, not including the pasta, per person.

Bacchus' Ratatouille Niçoise

1	medium eggplant
2–3	zucchini or summer squash
3	tablespoons oil
1	onion, finely chopped
1	clove garlic, crushed
1	16- or 18-ounce can no-salt tomatoes, including liquid
1	teaspoon chopped parsley
1	bay leaf
	Pepper to taste
½	cup grated Italian cheese (Parmesan, romano, or mozzarella)
2	tablespoons cold-pressed oil

1. Cube eggplant and squash.

2. Heat oil in deep frying pan and add onion. Cook until translucent or soft.

3. Add remaining ingredients except cheese; cover pan and cook on low heat for about 30 minutes.

4. Just before serving, sprinkle with cheese.

Serves 6, approximately 145 calories per serving.

Bacchus' Hawaiian Chicken Dinner

2	tablespoons oil
1	cup uncooked brown rice
1 ¼	cups chicken broth or stock
1 ¼	cups chicken, cut into small strips

2 cups chopped celery

1 cup coarsely chopped white or yellow onion

1 tablespoon low-sodium soy sauce

1 10-ounce can of natural juice-packed chunk pineapple, undrained

1. Heat frying pan and add 1 tablespoon oil and uncooked brown rice. Stir and brown lightly.

2. Pour browned rice into a 2-quart casserole, stirring in chicken broth or stock. Cover and bake in a preheated 350-degree oven for 1 hour, checking every 15 minutes and adding more broth if needed.

3. In a separate pan, heat remaining oil, then the chicken strips, and cook until the chicken turns white.

4. Add the celery and onion and cook until vegetables are slightly tender.

5. Add the soy sauce and pineapple with its juice; heat through and mix together with the rice mixture.

6. Replace all ingredients in the casserole and heat in oven an additional 5–10 minutes.

Serves 6, approximately 300 calories per serving.

CHAPTER VIII:

NUTRITION PLANS
PANCREAS VULNERABILITIES

Balanced Nutrition Plan For
Minerva • Aphrodite • Diana

Selective Diet: Low Sodium, Low Carbohydrate

Minerva, Aphrodite, and Diana function best on a diet low in saturated fats and carbohydrates, as this will help them to maintain good health.

A diet high in fats and sugars can lead to overweight or obesity and can heighten the pancreatic problems to which they are susceptible. Also, since their blood sugar levels may fluctuate when they're under stress, these goddesses should eat small amounts of food at frequent intervals.

Priority Foods

- Animal proteins: fish (especially fresh) of all kinds, lean beef and lamb, fowl of all kinds but those mentioned in "Avoidance Foods"
- Vegetables: green and yellow, all kinds, especially leafy green
- Fruits: all kinds
- Grains: oats, rye, bran, and whole-wheat
- Nuts and seeds: all kinds, especially sprouted seeds
- Oils: sunflower, soybean, sesame, corn, and safflower
- Dairy: low-fat milk, cottage cheese, yogurt, skim milk cheese

Limited Foods

Wine, beer, drinks with caffeine, dried fruits, brown rice, fresh tomatoes, corn, sweet potatoes, butter, ice milk, olives, and peanuts.

Avoidance Foods

Dark turkey meat, duck, pork, marbled meats, processed meats, fried food, ice cream, refined or processed sugars, carbonated beverages with sugar, chocolate, commercial pastries and candies, MSG (monosodium glutamate), preservatives, red food coloring, and hard liquor.

Vitamin and Mineral Requirements

One vitamin B-complex (50 mg.) with vitamin C, 10,000 I.U. vitamin A, 400 I.U. of vitamin D, and 400 I.U. vitamin E daily. (The 10,000 I.U. of vitamin A is the average recommended dose. You should not take more than this amount without consulting your physician.) An occasional digestive aid following a meal may be helpful.

Meal Timing

Up to six small meals a day. Snacks should be scheduled for times when your energy dips.

Morning meal ....between 6:30 and 8:30 a.m.
Midmorning snack ....between 10:30 and 11:30 a.m.
Midday meal ....between noon and 2:00 p.m.
Midafternoon snack ....between 2:30 and 3:30 p.m.
Evening meal ....between 5:30 and 7:30 p.m.
Late snack ....between 8:30 and 10:00 p.m.

Daily Instructions

- Drink four 8-ounce glasses of water daily.
- Avoid eating when emotionally stressed. Calm down first, then eat.
- Eat your heaviest meal in the middle of the day as often as possible.
- Be careful not to use food as a substitute for emotional insecurities.
- Elevate your feet and rest a half hour after the evening meal.

MINERVA • APHRODITE • DIANA
WEIGHT-MANAGEMENT CHART

Height (Without Shoes)	Desired Weight (Pounds) Small Frame	Medium Frame	Large Frame	Calorie Allowance for Maintained Weight
4' 10"	102 – 111	109 – 121	118 – 131	900 – 1000
11"	103 – 113	111 – 123	120 – 134	950 – 1100
5' 0"	104 – 115	113 – 126	122 – 137	1000 – 1200
1"	106 – 1 18	115 – 129	125 – 140	1050 – 1250
2"	108 – 121	118 – 132	128 – 143	1100 – 1300
3"	111 – 124	121 – 135	131 – 147	1150 – 1350
4"	114 – 127	124 – 138	134 – 151	1200 – 1400
5"	117 – 130	127 – 141	137 – 155	1250 – 1450
6"	120 – 133	130 – 144	140 – 159	1300 – 1500
7"	123 – 136	133 – 147	143 – 163	1350 – 1550
8"	126 – 139	136 – 150	146 – 167	1400 – 1600
9"	129 – 142	139 – 153	149 – 170	1450 – 1650
10"	132 – 145	142 – 156	152 – 173	1500 – 1700
11"	135 – 148	145 – 159	155 – 176	1550 – 1750
6' 0"	138 – 151	148 – 162	158 – 179	1600 – 1800

If you are a Minerva, Aphrodite, or Diana and want to know if you are the proper weight for your height and structure, refer to the above weight-management chart. This chart is based on standard insurance companies' data (Society of Actuaries and Association of Life Insurance Medical Directors of America, 1984).

The calorie allowances are for ages twenty-five to fifty-nine. These ages represent most women in the United States today. According to our statistics on these women, most tend to be of small bone structure, and tend to be overweight.

For those under twenty-five or over fifty-nine, the calorie allowances vary slightly from individual to individual, though in general more calories are needed in youth and fewer in the senior years, due to differences in life-style activities. (The calorie allowances indicated here are based on data from the N.I.H. National Institute on Aging, Baltimore, Maryland.)

SEVEN-DAY MENU PLAN
MINERVA • APHRODITE • DIANA

DAY 1 • WEIGHT LOSS
(approximately 900 calories)

Meal	Calories
BREAKFAST	
⅔ cup oatmeal	88
½ cup skim milk	45
1 fresh peach, sliced	40
Cup of coffee	—
	173
SNACK	
1 slice 7-grain bread	75
½ ounce skim milk cheese	35
Cup of Pero or herbal tea	—
	110
LUNCH	
3 ounces chicken cubes sautéed in 1 teaspoon sesame, oil, thyme, and soy bacon bits	200
½ cup boiled parslied potatoes with skins	60
½ cup steamed green beans	15
Hot herbal tea	—
	275

SNACK

4 Wheat Thins	40
½ cup cucumber slices	10
Perrier with lime slice	—
	50

DINNER

½ cup low-sodium V-8 juice	25
4 ounces broiled swordfish steak	135
1 cup baked zucchini with tarragon and 1 teaspoon sesame oil, sprinkled with sesame seeds	42
Salad of red and green leaf lettuce, scallions, green pepper rings, and alfalfa sprouts, with	20
2 tablespoons apple cider vinegar	5
Cup of decaffeinated coffee	—
	227

SNACK

4 carrot sticks	24
1 Norwegian Flatbread	20
	44

TOTAL CALORIES FOR THE DAY   879

DAY 2 • WEIGHT LOSS
(approximately 900 calories)

Meal	Calories
BREAKFAST	
1 poached egg	78
1 slice rye toast with	70
½ teaspoon unsalted butter	21
Cup of coffee	—
	169
SNACK	
⅔ cup of cauliflower and broccoli flowerets	30
Cup of Pero or hot herbal tea	—
	30
LUNCH	
3 ounces sliced roast beef	224
1 cup asparagus, steamed	33
1 slice sprouted-wheat bread	65
Cup of decaffeinated coffee	—
	322
SNACK	
8 unsalted roasted almonds	49
½ cup low-sodium V-8 juice	25
	74

DINNER

4 ounces freshwater trout broiled with	135
Almond slivers	42
1 cup green beans, steamed	36
Salad of cooked artichoke hearts, chives, green onions, and watercress with apple cider vinegar	50
¼ small canteloupe or ⅔ cup of mixed melon balls	30
Cup of hot comfrey tea	—
	293

SNACK

2 slices Melba toast	30
Hot water with lemon slice	—
	30

TOTAL CALORIES FOR THE DAY   918

DAY 3 • WEIGHT LOSS
(approximately 900 calories)

Meal	Calories

BREAKFAST

½ cup All-Bran cereal	90
½ cup skim milk	45
½ cup strawberries	26
	161

SNACK

½ cup each cucumber and zucchini slices with	20
2 tablespoons Cucumber Yogurt Dip (see Iris/Venus recipes)	20
Perrier with lime slice	—
	40

LUNCH

3 ounces chopped steak	190
½ cup Chinese snow peas and	30
Chopped sweet red pepper, sautéed in	10
1 teaspoon sesame oil	42
1 slice whole-grain bread	65
Cup of decaffeinated coffee	—
	337

SNACK

2 ounces low-sodium V-8 juice	25
2 whole-wheat crackers	40
	65

DINNER

4 ounces shellfish or 5 average shrimp (steamed, boiled, or baked)	100
Salad of cold artichoke heart, bibb lettuce, green pepper rings, alfalfa sprouts, and vinegar dressing	25
1 serving Natural Fruit Ambrosia*	90
Glass of herbal iced tea	—
	215

*See recipe.

SNACK

1 slice whole-wheat toast with	70
1 teaspoon honey	25
	95

TOTAL CALORIES FOR THE DAY   **913**

DAY 4 • WEIGHT MAINTENANCE
(approximately 1200 calories)

Meal	Calories
BREAKFAST	
½ cup oatmeal	66
½ cup skim milk	45
5 dried apricot halves	85
Cup of coffee	—
	196
SNACK	
1 slice Banana Bran Bread*	110
Cup of decaffeinated coffee or Pero	—
	110
LUNCH	
1 cup gazpacho soup	50
3 ounces lean roast lamb slices or small	
loin lamb chop	200
½ small baked potato with	
Mock Sour Cream*	80
1 cup chopped broccoli, steamed	36
Iced herbal tea with lemon	2
	368

*See recipe.

SNACK

1 Norwegian Flatbread	20
1 cup cucumber slices and celery stick	28
Cup of Postum	—
	48

DINNER

½ small broiled chicken	310
1 cup green beans, steamed with green onions	51
Salad of cooked artichoke hearts, chives, green pepper rings, and watercress, with	20
1 tablespoon oil, apple cider vinegar, and sesame seed dressing	80
½ large baked apple with cinnamon	38
Cup of hot herbal tea	—
	499

TOTAL CALORIES FOR THE DAY   1221

DAY 5 • WEIGHT MAINTENANCE
(approximately 1200 calories)

Meal	Calories

BREAKFAST

1 boiled egg	78
1 slice rye toast with	75
1 small pat of butter or margarine	36
4 ounces fresh orange juice	56
Cup of coffee	—
	245

SNACK

8-ounce cup of chicken broth with chives	53
½ cup cucumber slices and broccoli flowerets	20
	73

LUNCH

4 ounces broiled veal steak	340
½ cup boiled parslied potatoes with skins	60
½ cup spinach, steamed	20
1 slice sprouted-wheat bread	40
½ cup low-fat cottage cheese	86
Cup of decaffeinated coffee	—
	546

SNACK

¼ small cantaloupe	30
Perrier with lime slice	—
	30

DINNER

1 cup low-sodium V-8 juice	50
1 serving of Flounder Fillet Roll-Ups*	140
1 baked zucchini boat with tarragon and 1 teaspoon sesame oil sprinkled with sesame seeds	82
Salad of red and green leaf lettuce, alfalfa sprouts, scallions, green pepper rings, with	25
2 tablespoons apple cider vinegar	5
Cup of Postum or herbal tea	—
	302

TOTAL CALORIES FOR THE DAY   1196

*See recipe.

DAY 6 • WEIGHT MAINTENANCE
(*approximately 1200 calories*)

Meal	Calories
BREAKFAST	
1 cup Cream of Wheat	140
½ cup skim milk	45
½ cup strawberries (8 large, sliced)	28
Cup of Postum	—
	213
SNACK	
1 stone-ground wheat cracker	20
1 cup hot or cold apple cider	160
	180
LUNCH	
1 cup low-sodium V-8 juice	50
4 ounces broiled lean sirloin steak	250
1 cup green peas with pearl onions	82
1 slice whole-grain bread with	70
1 pat of unsalted butter	36
Cup of decaffeinated coffee	—
	488
SNACK	
4 ounces low-fat yogurt	70
DINNER	
1 cup vegetable soup	75
3 ounces Artichoke and Tuna Salad*	100
Salad of watercress, chives, bibb lettuce,	

*See recipe.

and green pepper rings with apple cider vinegar	25
1 fresh plum or peach	32
Cup of hot herbal tea	—
	232

TOTAL CALORIES FOR THE DAY   1183

DAY 7 • FUN DAY
(approximately 1600 calories)

Meal	Calories

BREAKFAST

1 scrambled egg with 1 teaspoon butter	111
1 Oatmeal Muffin*	125
½ cup mixed melon balls	72
Cup of coffee, decaffeinated or regular	—
	308

SNACK

1 6-ounce container of low-fat blueberry yogurt	190
Cup of Postum	—
	190

LUNCH

1 cup tomato bisque soup (made with skim milk)	150

*See recipe.

4 ounces fillet of sole with	90
Almond slivers	30
1 small baked potato with	104
2 tablespoons of chives and	
Mock Sour Cream*	21
1 cup steamed mixed vegetables	35
Cup of hot herbal tea with lemon	—
	430

SNACK

1 8-ounce diet soda	3
1 rice cake	36
1 tablespoon peanut butter	84
	123

DINNER

1 small Italian Pizza* garnished with	270
5 anchovy fillets	35
½ cup raw sliced mushrooms	10
½ cup diced green peppers	17
Tossed salad with carrots, cucumbers,	
radishes, spinach, and bibb lettuce, with	40
1 tablespoon creamy dressing	70
1 light beer (12 ounces)	110
	552

TOTAL CALORIES FOR THE DAY   1603

*See recipe.

RECIPES FOR MINERVA • APHRODITE • DIANA MEAL PLANNING

Diana's Artichoke and Tuna Salad

    1   10-ounce package frozen artichoke hearts
    1   6½-ounce can of drained, water-packed tuna
    1   teaspoon oil
        Apple cider vinegar to taste
        Basil to taste
        Fresh ground pepper to taste

1. Cook artichoke hearts as directed and drain.
   Cut in half if desired.

2. Place in serving bowl and toss with remaining ingredients.

3. Let marinate in refrigerator an hour or so. Then toss again and serve, or warm before serving if you wish.

Serves 2–3, approximately 100 calories per serving.

Minerva's Mock Sour Cream Topping

    ½   cup low-fat cottage cheese
    1   teaspoon skim milk powder
    1½   teaspoons lemon juice
        Chopped chives, parsley, or other herbs to taste

1. Combine all ingredients in blender. Process on medium-high speed until smooth and creamy.

2. Cover and chill thoroughly.

Yields about ½ cup, about 10 calories per tablespoon.

Minerva's Oatmeal Muffins

¼	cup soy flour
¾	cup whole-wheat flour
1½	teaspoons baking soda
1	cup rolled oats
½	teaspoon ground cinnamon
1	egg
1	cup plain low-fat yogurt
¼	cup honey
3	tablespoons oil or margarine

Optional:

½   cup raisins, currants, chopped apples, dried fruit, chopped nuts or seeds, mashed banana, or 1 cup fresh or frozen blueberries

1. Combine dry ingredients.

2. Beat together egg, yogurt, honey, and oil and add to flour mixture, stirring just enough to moisten.

3. Fold in one optional ingredient if desired.

4. Fill lightly greased muffin cups to make 12. Bake in a preheated 425-degree oven for about 10 minutes.

Approximately 125 calories each.

Diana's Banana Bran Bread

1	cup of whole-wheat flour
1	cup of soy flour
½	teaspoon baking powder

༄

½   cup bran flakes
2   tablespoons honey
1   whipped egg
½   cup skim milk
2   ripe bananas, mashed

1. In a medium-sized mixing bowl, combine all dry ingredients without sifting.

2. Slowly add honey, egg, milk, and bananas and blend until smooth.

3. Pour into a lightly greased loaf pan or muffin tin and bake in a preheated 350-degree oven for 50 minutes.

Approximately 90 calories per ½-inch slice or about 110 calories per medium-sized muffin.

Minerva's Italian Pizza

Pizza Dough:

1   cup soy flour
2   tablespoons bran flakes
2   cups whole-wheat flour
¾   teaspoon salt
2   tablespoons dry yeast
1¼   cups lukewarm water
1   teaspoon honey
¼   cup oil

1. Combine flours, salt, and bran flakes, and set aside.

2. Sprinkle dry yeast over surface of water. Add honey, and stir, and let soak for 10 minutes.

3. Mix in dry mixture and roll into a ball. Slowly add oil to surface of dough and knead until smooth and gummy.

4. Place dough in oiled bowl and cover with a damp cloth to rise double in size.

5. After one hour, push down and knead again. (Total approximate rising time: 2 hours.)

6. Divide dough into three balls and roll out to $\frac{1}{4}$-inch thickness for pizza tins. Pinch edges by folding crust under $\frac{1}{2}$ inch at edge of pan.

7. Top each pizza with 1 cup of sauce (see below) and 1 cup of shredded mozzarella cheese, along with your favorite toppings. Bake in 450-degree oven for 15 minutes.

Tomato Sauce:

1	cup chopped onions
3	cloves garlic, minced
2	green peppers, diced
4	cups canned tomatoes
1	6-ounce can tomato paste
2	tablespoons oil
2	teaspoons honey
2	tablespoons Italian seasonings

1. Combine all ingredients in a 2-quart pan.

2. Simmer over low heat for approximately 1 hour.

Divide each pie into 4 slices. Approximately 270 calories per slice.

Aphrodite's Flounder Fillet Roll-Ups

1   pound fresh spinach leaves
    Vegetable cooking spray
1   large onion, finely chopped
1   clove garlic, minced
1   tablespoon margarine or butter blend
4   flounder fillets (about ¼ pound each)
¾   teaspoon dried dill
¼   teaspoon pepper
1   lemon, sliced
¼   cup dry white wine
¼   cup water
2   tablespoons Parmesan cheese
1   tablespoon bread crumbs

1. Cut spinach leaves into thin strips and set aside.

2. Coat a large skillet with the cooking spray. Heat skillet and sauté onion and garlic on medium-high heat until just tender.

3. Melt margarine in skillet and add spinach strips and saute' until just tender.

4. Place about ¼ of the spinach strips on short end of each fillet. Roll up the fillets and place them seam side down into a small square baking dish.

5. Combine onion mixture, dill, and pepper. Spoon this mixture over and around the fish roll-ups. Top with the lemon slices.

6. Combine the wine and water. Pour this mixture around the fillets. Sprinkle with cheese and bread crumbs.

7. Cover and bake at 375 degrees for 15–20 minutes or until fillets flake easily with a fork.

Makes 4 servings at approximately 140 calories each.

Aphrodite's Natural Fruit Ambrosia

   2   small apples, sliced
   2   grapefruits, peeled and sectioned
  ½   cup unsweetened orange juice
2–3   tablespoons unsweetened, shredded coconut

1. Combine fruits and juice in a bowl and toss.

2. Chill covered in the refrigerator for an hour or so.

3. To serve, spoon into 6 dessert dishes and sprinkle with coconut.

Each serving is approximately 90 calories.

Balanced Nutrition Plan
for Atlas • Eros • Hermes

Selective Diet: Low Fat, Low Carbohydrate

Atlas, Eros, and Hermes function best on a diet low in saturated fats and carbohydrates, as this will help them to maintain good health. A diet high in fats and sugars can lead to overweight or obesity and can heighten the pancreatic problems to which they are susceptible. Also, since their blood sugar levels may fluctuate when they're under stress, these gods should eat small amounts of food at frequent intervals.

Priority Goods

- Animal proteins: fish (especially fresh) of all kinds, lean beef and lamb, fowl of all kinds but those mentioned in "Avoidance Foods"
- Vegetables: green and yellow, all kinds, especially leafy green
- Fruits: all kinds
- Grains: oats, rye, bran, and whole-wheat
- Nuts and seeds: all kinds, especially sprout seeds
- Oils: sunflower, soybean, sesame, corn, and safflower
- Dairy: low-fat milk, cottage cheese, yogurt, skim milk cheese

Limited Foods

Wine, drinks containing caffeine, dried fruits, eggs, brown rice, fresh tomatoes, corn, sweet potatoes, butter, ice milk, olives, and peanuts.

Avoidance Foods

Dark turkey meat, pork, marbled meats, processed meats, fried food, ice cream, duck, refined or processed sugars, carbonated beverages with sugar, chocolate, commercial pastries and candies, MSG (monosodium glutamate), preservatives, red food coloring, and hard liquor.

Vitamin and Mineral Requirements

One vitamin B-complex (50 mg.) with vitamin C, 10,000 I.U. of vitamin A, 400 I.U. of vitamin D, and 400 I.U. of vitamin E daily. (The 10,000 I.U. indicated for vitamin A is the average recommended dosage. You should not take more than this amount without consulting your physician.) Occasionally a digestive aid following meals may be helpful.

Meal Timing

Up to six small meals a day. Snacks should be scheduled for times when your energy dips.

Morning meal . . . . between 6:30 and 8:30 a.m.
Midmorning snack . . . . between 10:30 and 11:30 a.m.
Midday meal . . . . between noon and 2:00 p.m.
Midafternoon snack . . . . between 2:30 and 3:30 p.m.
Evening meal . . . . between 5:30 and 7:30 p.m.
Late snack . . . . between 8:30 and 10:30 p.m.

Daily Instructions

- Drink four 8-ounce glasses of water daily.

- Avoid eating when emotionally stressed. Calm down first, then eat.

- As often as possible, eat your heaviest meal in the middle of the day.

- Be careful not to use food as a substitute for emotional needs.

- Rest a half hour after the evening meal.

ATLAS • EROS • HERMES WEIGHT-MANAGEMENT CHART

Height (Without Shoes)	Desired Weight (Pounds) Small Frame	Medium Frame	Large Frame	Calorie Allowance for Maintained Weight
5' 4"	132 – 138	135 – 145	142 – 156	1500 – 1800
5"	134 – 140	137 – 148	144 – 160	1550 – 1850
6"	136 – 142	139 – 151	146 – 164	1600 – 1900
7"	138 – 145	142 – 154	149 – 168	1650 – 1950
8"	140 – 148	145 – 157	152 – 172	1700 – 2000
9"	142 – 151	148 – 160	155 – 176	1750 – 2050
10"	144 – 154	151 – 163	158 – 180	1800 – 2100
11"	146 – 157	154 – 166	161 – 184	1850 – 2150
6' 0"	149 – 160	157 – 170	164 – 188	1900 – 2200
1"	152 – 164	160 – 174	168 – 192	1950 – 2250
2"	155 – 168	164 – 178	172 – 197	2000 – 2300
3"	158 – 172	167 – 182	176 – 202	2050 – 2350
4"	162 – 176	171 – 187	181 – 207	2100 – 2500

If you are an Atlas, Eros, or Hermes and want to know if you are the proper weight for your height and weight, refer to the previous weight-management chart. This chart is based on standard insurance companies' data (Society of Actuaries and Association of Life Insurance Medical Directors of America, 1984).

The calorie allowances are for ages twenty-five to fifty-nine. (The calorie allowances indicated here are based on data from the N.I.H. National Institute on Aging, Baltimore, Maryland.)

According to our statistics, Atlas and Eros are usually medium framed, while Hermes is often small framed.

SEVEN-DAY MENU PLAN
ATLAS • EROS • HERMES

DAY 1 • WEIGHT LOSS
(approximately 1100 calories)

Meal	Calories
BREAKFAST	
1 slice fresh pineapple	44
1 cup cooked rolled oats	132
½ cup skim milk	45
Cup of decaffeinated coffee	—
	221
SNACK	
2 boiled or steamed shrimp	40
3 celery stalks	10
Cup of Postum	—
	50
LUNCH	
½ cup low-sodium V-8 juice	25

6-ounces roasted chicken breast (skin removed)	200
1 cup steamed green beans	31
½ baked acorn squash with cinnamon	86
1 slice 7-grain bread	70
Hot herbal tea	—
	412

SNACK

2 Norwegian Flatbread crackers	40
½ cup raw zucchini slices	10
Perrier with lime slice	—
	50

DINNER

1 bowl of vegetable soup	125
1 bran muffin (small), with	85
1 pat corn oil margarine	35
Salad of red and green leaf lettuce, watercress, red onion slices and green pepper rings with	40
1 tablespoon low-calorie Thousand Island dressing	25
Iced herbal tea with lemon	—
	310

SNACK

½ cup fruit cocktail (in natural juice)	37
2 Stone Wheat Thins	26
	63

TOTAL CALORIES FOR THE DAY　　1106

DAY 2 • WEIGHT LOSS
(approximately 1100 calories)

Meal	Calories
BREAKFAST	
1 poached egg	78
1 slice rye toast with	75
½ teaspoon unsalted butter	36
Cup of hot herbal tea	—
	189
SNACK	
8 ounces Chicken Broth*	50
1 Rye Melba Round	20
	70
LUNCH	
6 ounces broiled bluefish	135
1 cup of asparagus steamed (8 spears)	33
1 whole-wheat roll, with	90
1 teaspoon unsalted butter	36
Medium bunch of grapes	50
Cup of decaffeinated coffee	—
	344
SNACK	
1 cup low-sodium V-8 juice	50
2 celery stalks, stuffed with	
1 ounce skim milk cheese	70
	120

*See recipe.

DINNER

6 ounces bay scallops baked with	
stewed tomatoes, onion slices, and herbs	200
1 cup green beans steamed, with	
3 teaspoons almonds	68
Salad of cooked artichoke hearts, chives,	
pimentos, watercress, and	
Romaine lettuce, with	48
1 tablespoon low-calorie Italian dressing	8
Iced herbal tea with mint leaf	—
	324

SNACK

½ cup low-fat plain yogurt, on	60
½ cup red raspberries	28
	88

TOTAL CALORIES FOR THE DAY   1135

DAY 3 • WEIGHT LOSS
(approximately 1300 calories)

Meal	Calories

BREAKFAST

1 cup bran flakes cereal	104
¾ cup skim milk	66
½ cup fresh sliced peaches	33
Cup of decaffeinated coffee	—
	203

SNACK

½ sliced cucumber and	
½ cup raw broccoli, with	30
Green Goddess Dip*	60
2 whole-wheat crackers	40
Perrier with lime	—
	130

LUNCH

6 ounces broiled flounder	120
1 cup Chinese snow peas, sautéed in	30
½ teaspoon sesame oil	21
½ cup Bulgur Pilaf*	230
Iced herbal tea with lemon	—
	401

SNACK

1 fresh pear	112
1 cup Pero	—
	112

DINNER

4 ounces white turkey meat, in a	200
Whole-wheat pita bread with	150
Shredded carrots, lettuce, alfalfa	
sprouts, and onions	22
1 tablespoon low-calorie ranch dressing	16
½ cold artichoke with yogurt dressing	35
Perrier with lime slice	—
	423

*See recipe.

SNACK

1 cup mixed fruit sugar-free gelatin	40
Cup of hot herbal tea	—
	40

TOTAL CALORIES FOR THE DAY   1309

DAY 4 • WEIGHT MAINTENANCE
(approximately 1500 calories)

Meal	Calories

BREAKFAST

2 4-inch buckwheat cakes or	
½ cup cooked buckwheat (kasha)	208
1 pat unsalted butter	36
½ cup unsweetened applesauce and	
cinnamon topping	50
Cup of coffee	—
	294

SNACK

1 8-ounce glass skim milk	88
1 crisp rye bread	52
	140

LUNCH

6 ounces broiled lean sirloin steak	360
½ cup mashed potatoes with skim milk	69
1 cup steamed broccoli	40
Hot herbal tea	—
	469

SNACK

1 6-ounce glass carrot juice	50
2 celery stalks and 3 cucumber slices	18
	68

DINNER

1 bowl homemade Clam Chowder*	118
Spinach salad with mushrooms, sprouts, and	
½ hard-boiled egg	62
1 tablespoon sunflower seeds (hulled)	50
2 tablespoons vinaigrette dressing	40
2 whole-wheat breadsticks	76
1 serving Country Peach Cobbler*	80
Perrier with lime slice	—
	426

SNACK

1 6-ounce low-fat vanilla yogurt,	90
Topped with 3 chopped walnut halves	30
	120

TOTAL CALORIES FOR THE DAY   1517

DAY 5 • WEIGHT MAINTENANCE
(*approximately 1700 calories*)

Meal	Calories

BREAKFAST

½ grapefruit	42
1 soft-boiled egg	78
1 slice whole-wheat toast	75

*See recipe.

1 pat unsalted butter	36
Cup of coffee	—
	231

SNACK

1 8-ounce Strawberry Shake*	100
2 Norwegian Flatbreads	40
	140

LUNCH

1 Seafood Kabob*	150
1 cup steamed brown rice with herbs	130
½ cup steamed mixed vegetables	58
1 serving Country Peach Cobbler*	80
1 8-ounce glass mineral water	—
	418

SNACK

1 bran muffin with pecans (see Athena's recipe)	140
Cup of hot herbal tea	—
	140

DINNER

2 lean broiled lamb loin chops	250
1 medium baked potato with chives	130
1 teaspoon corn oil margarine	72
½ cup sliced boiled carrots	24
Salad of greens with sprouts	20
2 tablespoons vinaigrette dressing	40
1 light beer	120
	656

*See recipe.

SNACK

1 8-ounce glass skim milk	88
8 roasted almonds	112
	200

TOTAL CALORIES FOR THE DAY   1785

DAY 6 • WEIGHT MAINTENANCE
(approximately 1700 calories)

Meal	Calories

BREAKFAST

½ cup Grape-Nuts cereal	200
½ cup skim milk	44
10 sliced strawberries	37
1 tablespoon pure honey	64
Cup of decaffeinated coffee	—
	345

SNACK

1 cup raw broccoli and cauliflower flowerets	28
2 ounces Green Goddess Dip*	60
Cup of hot herbal tea	—
	88

LUNCH

1 serving Chicken à l'Orange*	215
½ cup diced, parslied potatoes (boiled in skin), with	59
1 pat unsalted butter	36

*See recipe.

½ cup steamed zucchini and onion slices	22
Salad of Boston lettuce, cucumber and carrot	
slices, radishes, and mushroom pieces	35
2 tablespoons low-calorie French dressing	30
Perrier with lime slice	—
	397

SNACK

1 cup V-8 juice on ice cubes, with	50
2 celery stalks	6
1 whole-grain rice cake (unsalted)	38
	94

DINNER

4 ounces broiled salmon steak	200
½ baked acorn squash	86
Asparagus Salad*	82
1 cup mixed melon balls	80
1 4-ounce glass Rhine wine (11% alcohol)	96
	544

SNACK

1 Red Delicious sliced apple	62
1½ ounces skim semisoft cheese	150
Iced herbal tea	—
	212

TOTAL CALORIES FOR THE DAY   1680

*See recipe.

DAY 7 • FUN DAY
(approximately 1800 calories)

Meal	Calories

BREAKFAST

1 cup fresh orange juice	120
1 scrambled egg	111
1 slice honey bran toast	85
1 pat corn oil margarine	36
3 ounces broiled round steak	156
Cup of coffee	—
	508

SNACK

2 celery stalks, stuffed with	6
2 tablespoons chunky peanut butter	160
Iced herbal tea with lime slice	—
	166

LUNCH

1 serving Lasagna Roll-Ups*	330
Tossed salad with romaine and escarole lettuce, red onion and cabbage slices, tomato wedges, watercress, and fresh dill	50
2 tablespoons of vinaigrette dressing	40
1 slice whole-wheat garlic toast	101
1 12-ounce light beer	120
	641

SNACK

1 cup low-calorie fruit gelatin, topped with	56
2 ounces vanilla low-fat yogurt	28
Cup of decaffeinated coffee	—
	84

*See recipe.

DINNER

1 cup beef consommé	32
1 6-ounce serving fillet of sole amandine (almond slivers)	120
1 broiled tomato with bread crumbs and herb topping	58
3 artichoke hearts on watercress	30
1 tablespoon tarragon vinegar and sesame oil dressing	40
	280

SNACK

Medium bunch white grapes	50
Cup of hot herbal tea with lemon wedge	2
	52

TOTAL CALORIES FOR THE DAY   **1731**

RECIPES FOR ATLAS • EROS • HERMES MEAL PLANNING

Atlas' Clam Chowder

6   cups water
1   16-ounce can of tomatoes
1   16-ounce package frozen mixed vegetables (or two cups fresh)
1   tablespoon safflower oil
1   cup diced potatoes (with skins on)
1   tablespoon mixed herbs (basil, thyme,

parsley, and sage)
1 bay leaf
Dash of salt and pepper
1 4-ounce can minced clams

1. Combine all ingredients, except clams, in a large cooking pot. Cover and cook for 30 minutes.

2. Drain clams and add to stew. Simmer 10 more minutes and serve.

(Thicken with arrowroot and water if desired.)

Approximately 80 calories a cup, or 118 calories a bowl.

Eros' Chicken Broth or Consommé

2 pounds chicken backs or wings or other
   pieces except necks
6 cups water
1 large onion, cubed
1 celery stalk
1 teaspoon celery flakes
½ teaspoon pepper
1 cup mixed fresh chopped chives,
   celery leaves, and parsley

1. Place all ingredients, except chives, celery leaves, and parsley in a large covered pot and stew for 1 hour.

2. Remove from heat and cool with lid ajar for 1 hour.

∾

3. Skim fat from surface. Then strain and stir in the chives, celery leaves, and parsley. Heat for 5–10 minutes, bringing to the boiling point just before serving. Sprinkle whole-wheat croutons on top.

Approximately 50 calories per bowl, with croutons.

Eros' Fancy Asparagus Salad

1¼	pounds fresh asparagus (cleaned, trimmed, and cut up)
2	tablespoons apple cider vinegar
2	tablespoons red wine vinegar
2	tablespoons water
3	tablespoons dried chopped chives
1–2	cloves garlic, crushed or minced
¼	teaspoon paprika
	Watercress
1	hard-boiled egg

1. Steam asparagus 5–8 minutes, then place in a shallow casserole dish.

2. Mix together the vinegars, water, chives, garlic, and paprika and mix very well. Pour this mixture over the asparagus.

3. Chill for several hours.

4. When ready to serve, layer the watercress on a platter or shallow serving dish. Arrange the cut asparagus on top, pour the dressing over all. Grate the egg over the asparagus. Serve.

Serves 4, approximately 82 calories per serving.

Hermes' Companion Green Goddess Dip

½ cup plain low-fat yogurt
2 scallions (tops included, and chopped
   into 1-inch pieces)
1 tablespoon apple cider vinegar
1 garlic clove, minced
½ cup chopped watercress
½–1 teaspoon mixed herbs
   (tarragon, rosemary, dill, and coriander)
1 cup safflower mayonnaise

1. Combine all ingredients in blender and run on medium speed until smooth and creamy.

2. Place in a tightly covered container and refrigerate until ready to use. Keeps for about one week.

Approximately 30 calories per heaping tablespoon.

Atlas • Eros • Hermes' Bulgur Pilaf

1 tablespoon safflower oil
2 scallions with tops, chopped
½ cup chopped celery
½ cup chopped mushrooms
1 minced garlic clove
1 cup uncooked bulgur (cracked wheat)
2 cups Eros's chicken broth (*see recipe*)
½ teaspoon herbal blend seasoning
   Cayenne pepper to taste

1. Heat oil in skillet. Saute' onions, celery, mushrooms, and garlic until soft.

2. Stir in bulgur and lightly brown.

3. Add chicken broth and seasonings and bring to a boil.

4. Reduce heat, cover, and simmer for 15 minutes. Stir occasionally and fluff with fork when all the liquid is absorbed. Serve immediately.

Makes 4 servings, approximately 230 calories each.

Hermes' Lasagna Roll-ups

1	8-ounce box lasagna noodles
1	10-ounce box frozen chopped spinach
1	15-ounce container skim milk ricotta cheese
8	ounces grated mozzarella cheese
1	teaspoon basil, or more to taste
1	teaspoon oregano, or more to taste
$\frac{1}{8}$–$\frac{1}{4}$	teaspoon nutmeg
3	cups tomato sauce, stewed tomatoes, or combination of both
1/4	cup grated Parmesan cheese

1. Cook noodles according to package directions; drain and rinse.

2. Drain and press excess water from thawed spinach.

3. Combine the spinach with the cheeses (except Parmesan) and seasonings.

4. Spread about ⅔–½ cup spinach mixture lengthwise down each noodle and roll up like a jelly roll.

5. Spoon a small amount of sauce to cover bottom of the casserole dish and place the lasagna roll-ups in a single layer.

6. Top with remaining sauce. Sprinkle with Parmesan cheese, cover, and bake at 350 degrees for 30–40 minutes.

Makes 8 servings, approximately 330 calories each.

Atlas' Seafood Kabobs

1	8-ounce can pineapple chunks with natural juice
1–2	tablespoons Dijon mustard
1	tablespoon low-sodium soy sauce
1	pound medium-sized shrimp, peeled and deveined
½–¾	pound scallops
1	large green pepper, cut into squares
12	cherry tomatoes
½	pound fresh mushrooms

1. Drain pineapple and save juice.

2. Combine juice, mustard, and soy sauce in bowl. Add seafood and marinate in refrigerator for several hours, tossing occasionally.

3. Remove seafood and alternate it with the vegetables and pineapple on four skewers.

4. Brush marinade over each skewer and broil several minutes on each side, brushing again with sauce occasionally.

Serves 4, approximately 150 calories each.

Eros' Chicken À L'Orange

4	chicken breasts with skins removed
1⅓	cups orange juice
2	tablespoons dry white wine
1	tablespoon honey
1	scallion, thinly sliced
1	tablespoon whole-wheat pastry flour
1½	teaspoons grated or minced orange peel
½	medium orange, thinly sliced

1. Preheat oven to 350 degrees.

2. Arrange chicken in a covered casserole dish.

3. Combine orange juice, wine, honey, scallions, flour, and orange peel in a small saucepan and bring to a boil while stirring constantly.

4. Pour juice mixture over the chicken. Cover and bake ½ hour.

5. Uncover and bake an additional ½ hour, basting occasionally.

6. Top with orange slices and serve.

Serves 4, approximately 215 calories per serving.

Atlas' Country Peach Cobbler

    2   cups sliced fresh or frozen peaches

    1   tablespoon honey

    ⅓   cup honey graham cracker crumbs

    ½   teaspoon cinnamon

    ½   teaspoon pumpkin pie spice

    2   teaspoons margarine, melted

1. In a small casserole dish, layer the peaches.

2. Combine graham cracker crumbs, spices, honey, and margarine together and drizzle over top of peaches.

3. Bake about ½ hour in a 300-degree oven.

Makes 4 servings, approximately 80 calories per serving.

Hermes' Strawberry Shake

    1   pint fresh strawberries (or 1 10-ounce package, frozen unsweetened strawberries)

    1   cup skim milk

    1   cup plain yogurt

    2   tablespoons pure honey

    ½   teaspoon vanilla extract

    1½   cups crushed ice

          Pinch of mint flakes and wheat germ for topping

1. Combine ingredients in a blender and process until frothy.

2. Add more ice if needed and blend some more.

3. Serve with wheat germ and mint topping.

Serves 1, approximately 100 calories per serving.

CREATIVE MEAL PLANNING TECHNIQUES

To create your own menu:

1. Start with your choice of animal protein, so you can begin your calorie calculations with the largest number and add the smaller amounts to it.

2. Add any vegetables you want.

3. Select a grain and cereal product or some type of bread or cracker.

4. Add dairy products.

5. Select fruits, dried or fresh, and nuts or seeds.

6. Add oils, salad dressings, and sweets to enhance the flavor of your food.*

7. Include condiments, spices, and beverages to complete the meal.

*Be conservative with these items, since they can be high in calories. For instance, you may want to save your oil selection for a salad dressing instead of using it for cooking.

PREPARATION HINTS

Food Color

You can use an awareness of food color to help you create attractive and nutritious meals. When selecting from your list of priority foods, try to include as many different colors as possible. Not only will this help you create a more visually appealing menu, it will also ensure that you eat a variety of vitamins and minerals.

Stir-Fry or Sauté

Stir-frying involves rapidly cooking thin pieces of meat or vegetables in a small amount of oil to seal in freshness and flavor. For this cooking method you should use a skillet or wok, heat your oil until hot (but not smoking), then add any spices you choose—ginger root, garlic, or onion. It is best to begin with the meat, allowing the oil to cook it until it is brown, then add the vegetables and cover the skillet or wok and let them steam until cooked. The complete process takes about five to ten minutes. You may use herbs or soy sauce for additional flavor.

Broil or Bake

Broiling or baking means cooking without oil in an oven, usually on a rack about four inches from the heat source. Broiling works better than baking for thicker cuts of meat. For both broiling and baking, you should preheat your oven to ensure that your food cooks at a consistent temperature. Meat will then brown on the outside without overcooking on the inside.

Poach or Boil

Simmering fish, poultry, or vegetables in a seasoned liquid is a low-calorie method of preparing food. For best results, pour your poaching liquid in a saucepan, add fish or chicken, herbs and spices, and heat to boiling. Reduce the heat, and let your food simmer until it is cooked.

Steam

The ideal way to prepare vegetables so you lock in nutrients and flavors is to steam them over rapidly boiling water. Metal steamers are inexpensive, but you may use a colander instead. Ideally you should use a two- to three-quart saucepan with two to three inches of water. Heat the water to boiling, then place the vegetables in the rack and cover the pan with a tightly fitting lid. Steaming will take five to twenty minutes, depending on the size and type of vegetable being cooked, and your taste for soft or crisp veggies.

SUGGESTED SUBSTITUTIONS

- Oat bran or cracked wheat in place of white bread
- Whole-grain spaghetti in place of white pasta
- Honey in place of sugar
- Hot water and lemon slice or herbal teas instead of tea or coffee
- Apple cider in place of wine, both for drinking and cooking
- Fruit in place of other desserts
- Frozen yogurt in place of ice cream

Conclusion

THE POWER TO HEAL SELF

YOUR DIVINE BIRTHRIGHT GIVES YOU an indestructible healing power. You inherit two natures, a physical and a spiritual. Your spiritual nature defined is composed of subatomic energy, held together in a form termed "soul." The soul, with its own higher intelligence, entwines itself to the physical body through the central nervous system at specific points, or energy vortices, termed *chakras*. At these energy points, higher (spiritual) and lower (physical) intelligences come together, affecting every cell in your body.

Because Creative Wellness deals with the total person, I have chosen to close this book with an explanation of your dual nature, and an understanding of the special spiritual virtues that you, in reality, possess. Each one of you has within your psyche a soul that entered your body before birth and leaves at the moment of death. You have the responsibility to search for and to know this part of yourself in order to know who you are. You can open and attune to your chakras through meditation and prayer.

Famous physicians, such as Dr. Kubler Ross and Dr. Raymond Moody, have already opened the consciousness of science to explore deeper meanings into life and death itself. Both researchers have documented innumerable cases of life's existence after death and the continued intelligence of the soul.

∾

Since our physical bodies age daily, we are each challenged to live our full life's potential. We need to exist as if we are the living temples of the Holy Spirit. We need to get in touch with our individual soul and discover our place in the universe. We are destroying ourselves, not with a bomb, but with stress.

Some of the destructive stresses to our physical nature are not our inherited parental genes, rather, they are what we attract to and create for ourselves. We pollute our environment, and are unaware as to how we can protect ourselves from the pollution. We eat unnecessary poisonous chemicals, and don't know how to detoxify ourselves. And, most of all, we break down our inner chemical balance from worry, anxiety, negative attitudes, and destructive habits.

It's now time for us to become aware of our own inner power to combat stress. Each of us has untapped creative resources from our spirit within that, if used properly, can help us overcome almost any obstacle, including death.

There are many alternative therapies that we can use to protect our sensitivities. I would like to suggest to you a number of ways that you can take responsibility to help yourself to deal with your sensitivities:

- You can begin by taking classes in self-help care, particularly in the areas of alternative healing.

- See a body worker, such as, a chiropractor, and massage therapist, or an energy balancer—a polarity or Reiki healer—on a regular basis. Have yearly checkups by your physician.

- Get involved in community activities for collective or individual social improvement, or support groups sponsored by church or community services. Involvements help you to become socially conscious.

- Share your mystical and psychic interests and experiences with friends and coworkers. Seek out teachers and instructors who can aid your spiritual insight and empowerment. But, be careful to find only those who wish to be of service—not self-focused gurus or occult leaders.

- Seek always to find your own personal relationship with your Creator and to live as a child of God.

I have witnessed many wonderful happenings over the years, some of which could even be called faith miracles. All have had one thing in common: They involved a person calling on his or her own inner strength when there was no other place to turn. These people drew *the power* necessary to cope with their problem from their intangible spiritual nature within themselves. It is to this side of ourselves that we must turn when we feel alone, unloved, forgotten, or even incomprehensibly burdened with stress.

This is your *divine birthright*—your personal access to your own healing power. As a god or goddess, you have the strength to fight the seemingly unbearable and to attain the seemingly unattainable. All it takes is faith, hope in yourself, and love of your total being.

As your personality profiles have shown you, you have innumerable attributes that you need only acknowledge and develop. Once cultivated, you will be particularly blessed with the use of these special gifts to help both yourself and others. You will become a transformer and make a difference in the world. You will become one of the points of light that will raise consciousness and illumine society. Be creative and well caring for your whole self—body, mind, and spirit.

Special Attributes of the Goddesses

Athena	Sensitivity and humility
Artemis	Compassion and understanding
Iris	Courage and perseverance
Venus	Forgiveness and personal freedom
Minerva	Wisdom and self-acceptance
Aphrodite	Patience and self-management
Diana	Confidence and independence

Special Attributes of the Gods

Apollo	Generosity and sensitivity
Mercury	Tolerance and compassion
Neptune	Patience and fortitude
Bacchus	Temperance and perseverance
Atlas	Confidence and self-awareness
Eros	Self-assuredness and dependability
Hermes	Self-security and openness

RECOMMENDED READING

FOR MIND/BODY

The Healer Within, Steven Locke, M.D. & Douglas Colligan.
E.P. Dutton, 1987.
Love, Medicine & Miracles , Bernie S. Seigel, M.D. Harper & Row, 1986.
The Power Is Within You, Louise L. Hay. Hay House, 1991.
You Can Heal Your Life, Louise L. Hay. Hay House, 1989.

FOR NUTRITION

The Essential Guide to Vitamins and Minerals, Elizabeth Somer, M.A., R.D.
Harper Collins, 1992.
Great Recipes for Good Health, The Reader's Digest Association.
Reader's Digest, 1988.
The Healing Foods, Patricia Hausman & Judith Benn Hurley.
Rodale Press, 1989.
Microwave Lite Menu Cookbook, The Editors of Microwave Times.
Contemporary Books, 1986.

Weight Watchers Healthy Life-Style Cookbook, Weight Watchers International, 1991.

FOR NATURAL SUPPORTS

The Complete Book of Essential Oils & Aromatherapy, Valerie Anne Worwood. New World Library, 1991.
The Language of Color, Dorothee L. Mella. Warner Books, 1988.
Stone Power, Dorothee L. Mella. Warner Books, 1986.
Vibrational Medicine, Richard Gerber, M.D. Bear & Co., 1988.

FOR FURTHER STUDY

The Breath of Life, George Ellis. New Castle Publishing, 1992.
Goddesses in Every Woman, Jean Shinoda Bolen, M.D. Harper & Row, 1984.
The Sivananda Companion to Yoga, Lucy Lidell. Fireside Books, 1983.
T'ai-chi Ch'uan, Cheng Man-Ch'ing. North Atlantic Books, 1981.

For further information, or for additional help, please write to:

Creative Wellness
c/o NIMO Systems, Ltd.
P.O. Box 3872
Reston, VA 22090

The Printed Voice is a new company formed on cooperative principles between authors and publisher. The Printed Voice is committed to serving authors creative process, changing the world one voice at a time. For a complete list of titles, please write to:

The Printed Voice
98 Main Street No. 538
Tiburon, CA 94920